"This book will make you homesick for places you've never been. But more than that, it will make you homesick for the people you love. This book is about how going home sometimes looks like uprooting ourselves from everything familiar in order to make our home in the heart of someone else. It is a hard journey. But as Kate so tenderly teaches, it is the truest happy ending."

LISA-JO BAKER, best-selling author of *Never Unfriended* and *Surprised by Motherhood*

"The best memoirs either pull the reader into the author's compelling story or draw the author's universal truths into the reader's story. *A Place to Land* deftly manages both. Despite the many challenges she faces, Kate presses on, urging us by example to do the same. In the end, her thoughtful conclusions about longing and belonging may well become our own."

LIZ CURTIS HIGGS, best-selling author of *Bad Girls of the Bible*

"Kate Motaung has written an honest and touching memoir. *A Place to Land* will be an inspiration to anyone who is wrestling with God through life's unexpected losses."

LYNN AUSTIN, author of *Where We Belong*

"Even if we haven't shuttled between oceans or traveled the lonely, dark roads of death and parents' divorce, like Kate Motaung, we have all experienced home as longing and loss. Can we find hope in our seasons of suffering? *A Place to Land* confidently answers yes, lifting our eyes beyond this fragile, temporary life to a better world to come."

JEN POLLOCK MICHEL, author of *Keeping Place* and *Teach Us to Want*

"Kate Motaung draws readers into the spacious place of God's never-ending love. Into a place where we can land, forever."

EMILY T. WIERENGA, author of *Atlas Girl* and *Making It Home* and founder of The Lulu Tree (www.thelulutree.com)

"One of the paradoxes of the Christian faith is that we find our home by embracing our identities as wa... ...ply, to live in exile. Kate Motaung ... ...ring her own raw story of loss, long... ...our home. For anyone haunted by ... ...will serve as both a comfort and a c... ...one, true home."

D1214283

SHARON HODDE MILLER, author of *Free of Me: Why Life Is Better When It's Not about You*

"Followers of Jesus know we are on a journey toward a sweet reunion and a heavenly home. Kate Motaung's winsome memoir of longing and loss is illumination for the road. *A Place to Land* shines the light of Scripture on our common desire to feel at home somewhere in the world, and the truth revealed is like Michigan chocolate chip cookies served with South African Rooibos tea. Bittersweet but delicious."

CHRISTIE PURIFOY, author of *Roots and Sky: A Journey Home in Four Seasons*

"*A Place to Land* is a hopeful narrative of a home lost and found, and a gentle reminder of our Companion all along the way."

ASHERITAH CIUCIU, founder of One Thing Alone Ministries and author of *Unwrapping the Names of Jesus: An Advent Devotional* and *Full: Food, Jesus and the Battle for Satisfaction*

"I've heard it said believers are so heavenly minded they're of no earthly good. Kate's compelling story proves the opposite. It's exactly because she's learned to take the long view—living with eternity in mind—that her impact in this world is so startlingly powerful."

DALENE REYBURN, author of *Dragons and Dirt: The Truth about Changing the World—and the Courage It Requires* and *Walking in Grace: 366 Inspirational Devotions for an Abundant Life*

"This is for all of us who ache for solid ground in between *what if* and *now what*. You will land closer to the hope of your eternal home as you unpack Motaung's moving memoir."

KATIE M. REID, author of *Made Like Martha*

"*A Place to Land* is a page turner. Kate lifted my eyes and recalibrated my heart to long for home."

VIVIAN MABUNI, speaker and author of *Warrior in Pink: A Story of Cancer, Community, and the God Who Comforts*

"This book is a must-read for anyone walking through grief."

ASHLEIGH SLATER, author of *Braving Sorrow Together* and *Team Us*

"Let Kate's story break your heart, and then let the truth that pours out of these pages settle into your soul—that only eternal life with Christ will forever satisfy your deepest needs for belonging and home."

KELLY GIVENS, editor of iBelieve.com

"*A Place to Land* gave me the courage to forgive and trust in the Lord to work His good in our difficulties."

KRISTIE ANYABWILE, pastor's wife, mom, Bible teacher

KATE MOTAUNG

a story of longing & belonging

Discovery House.
from Our Daily Bread Ministries

A Place to Land: A Story of Longing and Belonging

© 2018 by Kate Motaung

All rights reserved.

Discovery House is affiliated with Our Daily Bread Ministries, Grand Rapids, Michigan.

Requests for permission to quote from this book should be directed to: Permissions Department, Discovery House, P.O. Box 3566, Grand Rapids, MI 49501, or contact us by email at permissionsdept@dhp.org.

All Scripture quotations, unless otherwise indicated, are taken from the Holy Bible, New International Version,® NIV,® Copyright © 1973, 1978, 1984 by Biblica, Inc.™ Used by permission of Zondervan. All rights reserved worldwide. zondervan.com. Some quotations taken from the Holy Bible, New International Version,® NIV.® Copyright © 2011 by Biblica, Inc.™ The "NIV" and "New International Version" are trademarks registered in the United States Patent and Trademark Office by Biblica, Inc.™

Scripture quotations marked ESV are from the ESV® Bible (The Holy Bible, English Standard Version®), copyright © 2001 by Crossway, a publishing ministry of Good News Publishers. Used by permission. All rights reserved.

Interior design by Rob Williams, InsideOutCreativeArts.com

ISBN: 978-1-62707-662-3

Printed in the United States of America
First printing in 2018

TO SARAH

FOR EVERYTHING

Kate Motaung

Colossians 3:2

CONTENTS

PROLOGUE

September 2011

I shimmied my way into the middle seat, disappointed that I didn't get the aisle. I guess I should have expected it, considering I had only booked my flight from South Africa to the United States that same morning. The woman who scored the aisle seat next to me waited for the click of my seat belt before launching into the obligatory small talk.

"Are you heading home?" she asked.

I hesitated—a little too long. Then finally, "Um . . . I, uh . . . yeah. Well, no. Uh . . . I'm not sure."

I wouldn't have blamed her if she'd flagged down the flight attendant right then. "Excuse me, ma'am, but this girl doesn't know where she's going."

"My mom died this morning," I blurted, the aircraft still grounded on the Cape Town runway. The previous twelve hours had soaked up all the tears I had in me, and I was left with only the sunken hollow of my bloodshot eyes. The kind woman gushed condolences before I could attempt to redeem my earlier fumble.

"I've been living in Africa for the past nine years, but my mom just died in my hometown in Michigan. So, I guess I'm heading home. But not really. I mean, my husband and kids are still here in Cape Town, so . . ."

I realized the answer to her original question hadn't become any clearer for either one of us.

CHAPTER 1

ENOUGH

*"Did we in our own strength confide,
our striving would be losing . . ."*

—Martin Luther, "A Mighty Fortress Is Our God"

Three Months Earlier, June

Our seventh wedding anniversary fell on Father's Day that year—the same day I took our three kids and left my husband standing alone in the Cape Town International Airport. Was I leaving home or going home? Even after nine years of living in South Africa, I wasn't sure.

For my kids, it was an adventure. A holiday. One big in-flight movie marathon in a transatlantic personal theatre. For me, it was a final, desperate fling of the life ring to my mom, who was barely keeping her head above water in the turbulent seas of cancer and chemotherapy.

I was scared—and bothered by my unstable nerves. Why should I be afraid of visiting my own mother? Deep down, I feared the unknown. I had no idea what to expect. Living over eight thousand miles away was agonizing in many ways, but it had protected me from the reality of her pain.

After thirty-six hours of travel, I herded my brood and our bulging suitcases down the arrivals corridor in Grand Rapids, Michigan. I scanned the crowd, searching for a familiar face until my eyes locked on my younger sister, Sarah, and her life-giving smile. I breathed a sigh of exhaustion and relief, and then laughed as my kids attacked their beloved aunt with squeals, hugs, and an immediate flood of words. I pushed through their run-on sentences to hug my sister long and hard—the kind of embrace that stalls time and whispers knowledge of shared burdens.

I wanted to apologize for leaving her to take care of Mom by herself, to thank her for carrying the load I should have helped her shoulder. Instead, I told her how good it was to see her—a salve to my throbbing soul. Just by being together again, I felt more complete. And yet, a hole remained: Mom should have been there too. On my other visits over the past nine years, Mom would practically run through the arrivals terminal, unable to contain her excitement. This time, she was too sick to even endure a forty-five-minute car ride to the airport.

We loaded up the vehicle Sarah borrowed just to fit all of us and our paraphernalia for six weeks and drove to our hometown of Holland, Michigan, five voices vying to be heard the whole way. As Sarah pulled into the parking lot of Mom's rental condo, I felt myself suck in a breath of apprehension. I had last seen my mom eight months prior, for her fifty-ninth birthday. Not counting the multiple Skype calls, the kids hadn't seen her for two years. What would we find inside?

We climbed the steps and corralled my exhausted but excited children through the doorway. I turned and found Mom sitting on the couch—smaller than I'd ever seen her. It seemed as though her spirit was waging war with her flesh, as if she could will her body to strengthen. I could see how she longed to stand up and squeeze love into our marrow but was too weak to move from her sunken position. She looked up at us with a feeble smile, and I saw the sun rise in her bloodshot eyes. By bringing her grandchildren, I had ushered in the dawn.

I tried to mask my shock. With great effort, I lowered my raised eyebrows and widened my smile. Mom's physical state had deteriorated drastically since my last visit. She was fading away, like a waning moon. I bent down to hug her, pretending I wasn't shaken that she couldn't rise to greet me. It was so unlike her.

Before, she would've lugged our suitcases into the house herself before hurrying into the kitchen to reveal a plate of freshly baked chocolate chip cookies. This time, when she did stand up, she relied heavily on a borrowed walker and even then, her arms shook as she shuffled along on numb feet. Her breathing was labored even with the help of oxygen tubes. If I hadn't been trying to stay strong for the sake of Mom and my kids, I would've collapsed into tears. I wanted to tell God it was too much. That I couldn't handle it any more.

The kids couldn't get enough of their grandma, asking question after question about toys and books she had gathered for their arrival. I could see that Mom longed to get up and play, to read stories together, and pretend to be the customer at the kids' imaginary store. Instead, she stayed put, asking the kids to bring things to her so she didn't have to move.

Once the initial excitement of our reunion had settled down a bit, we called my husband, Kagiso, on Skype to tell him we had arrived safely. He saw Mom on the webcam and asked, "How are you?"

Although she was visibly struggling to move, she answered, "Well, I've had a few rough days, but now that Kate and the kids are here, I'm *perfect!*" I looked at her, slack-jawed by her choice of adjective. I thought, *This woman in her current condition is about as far from perfect as a person can get.*

After a while, I could tell that Mom's energy was dwindling. Just talking seemed to be a strain, even while sitting in a chair. I made eye contact with Sarah. "Let's go drop off our suitcases at your house. Then maybe we could go say hi to Dad before we come back here for dinner."

Sarah agreed. The kids and I lined up to give my mom hugs and kisses good-bye. "Get some rest," I told her. "We'll be back to make supper in a couple of hours."

That evening, Sarah and her husband Kent drove separately to Mom's condo. When the kids and I pulled back into the complex, we saw that Sarah and Kent had arrived a few minutes before us. "Go ahead and run upstairs,"

I told my kids, knowing that my sister and brother-in-law were already inside. My aching, exhausted body lagged behind. As soon as I heard the tone of Kent's voice in the corridor, I knew something was wrong: "Let's just wait out here for a while." I caught the tail end as he whisked my daughter and two sons back into the hallway. With renewed adrenaline, I scaled the flight of stairs to see what was going on.

"Sarah walked in and found your mom lying on the bathroom floor," Kent whispered so the kids couldn't hear. "She was conscious, but unable to get up. We think she'd been there for a while."

Kent and I did our best to distract the kids in the hallway while Sarah helped Mom get cleaned up and back to the couch. Kent passed the time by asking the kids brain teasers, riddles, and trivia questions while I bit my nails and pretended to pay attention. Eventually Sarah swung open the door with a fake smile, and the evening continued as normally as possible. My sister later confided that Mom fell, even while using her walker, and decided not to press the emergency button around her neck because she didn't want to interrupt our time with Dad.

We didn't speak of the incident out loud again.

That first night, after traveling alone with three kids across six time zones, I sank into the underinflated air mattress at Sarah and Kent's house and quickly slipped into unconsciousness. What seemed like days later, a shadowy figure shook me awake. My weighted eyelids fought to open, but in the darkness, I could only discern an even darker form—it was talking, but my clouded mind couldn't process the message: "Mom fell. *Again.* I'm going over there to spend the night at her condo."

Was this a nightmare? *It had to be.* This could not be happening now. The shadow vanished, and I let my head sink back into the feather pillow. But my mind would not rest.

Shuffling downstairs, I found my brother-in-law pacing the moonlit sun porch. "Is this for real?" I asked, my mind still shrouded by a fog of fatigue. He exhaled loudly, a pressurized helium tank deflating. Then reluctantly, "Yep. It is."

The next day earned a spot in the Top Ten Worst Days of My Life. Despite my hopes, I woke up to the stark reality that the previous night had, in fact, *not* been a bad dream. Mom had fallen. Twice. Even while using a walker, with an emergency call button dangling from a lanyard around her neck. Clearly it wasn't safe for her to live alone anymore. We had to do something. A nagging feeling pricked my spine—*things are about to get much worse.* After all my longing to be present, to be on the same continent, in the same town—when I finally found myself there, I wasn't sure I could handle it.

Sarah came home to shower and get clean clothes after spending the night at Mom's. Since Kagiso was still in South Africa, Kent graciously took on the monumental task of feeding, bathing, and entertaining my three kids all day, while Sarah and I embarked on an even more difficult assignment.

We drove together back to the condo, a thick sense of foreboding in the car. When we arrived, Mom was lying in bed, but awake. Sarah and I knelt on either side of her queen-sized mattress, two pieces of bread sandwiching her like we used to when she read to us as little girls—though the blonde heads had since become more like whole wheat . . . or maybe even rye. With bare knees on the carpet and bent elbows touching the sheet, my unintentional prayerlike posture seemed appropriate. God knew my every breath in those moments was a plea for help.

The following minutes unraveled as one of those scenes in the movie of life where the camera zooms in and the background music crescendos. Emotions pulsed, audible and palpable. After four consecutive years of nonstop chemotherapy treatments, Mom's body had had enough. All three of us knew it, but nobody wanted to admit defeat. Speaking the words aloud would seal the deal. Game over.

"I just don't know how much longer I can keep going," Mom confessed, her voice catching as she looked straight ahead at the blank wall.

I summoned every ounce of bravery I could muster—and found myself lacking. The lump in my throat kept the words caged in my chest, banging on the gate to be free. I longed to lavish verbal praise on my mom for her strength—not just in the cancer years, but in every year since my dad left. I wanted to tell her how much I admired her perseverance, the way she endured hardship and trials without complaint, the way she just kept going, no matter what. Until that morning, *stopping* didn't exist in her vocabulary. Cancer's ability to place it there made me rage.

Mom had been holding on, valiantly enduring countless side effects, and now the chemo itself was killing her. As it was, she had no feeling in her hands or feet from the neuropathy. The tingling sensation spread farther with every treatment. She took eighteen different prescription medications every day at various times—some for specific ailments, others to counter the side effects of the first batch of drugs. Yet, if she stopped chemo while the cancer ravaged through her bones, lungs, and liver, we all knew what would happen.

The three of us sniffled and dabbed tears with crumpled tissues, sighing loud heaves in harmony with the rhythm of Mom's oxygen tank. An unspoken consensus. My eyes met Sarah's, and I saw the same answer: we'd reached the end.

I watched the tug-of-war wage in Mom's soul. She took a deep breath through the tubes in her nose, and surrendered.

"Okay," she exhaled. "I'll call the oncology office and tell them I won't be coming in for my treatment. I'm going to stop the chemo." The words came out feeble and resigned. Laced with reluctance. And they just about knocked the wind out of me.

I caught a glimpse of blue sky through the window and wanted to make like a bird and fly away. When I saw there was no way to escape, I let my shoulders fall and realized there was no place I'd rather be. I found myself echoing Jesus's prayer from the cross: "Father, if you are willing, take this cup from me; yet not my will, but yours be done" (Luke 22:42, NIV 2011). If Mom had to walk through this fire, I wanted to be by her side.

"I'm not afraid to die," Mom announced. She knew the One in whom she trusted and held a deep and unmoving confidence in His promise to carry her home (1 Tim. 1:12). Resolve mounted in her voice, even as tears dripped down her cheeks. "I just feel bad for you girls." She knew the years ahead of us were going to hurt, finishing our days as motherless daughters.

That awful morning, God gave me a fresh awareness that she hadn't been clinging to life for herself. She hadn't fought for nine years for her own sake. Her determination swelled up from something far beyond herself. She was fighting for *us*. And between the tears, I saw Jesus. How He didn't live His life for Himself. How He gave it up, every day of it, as a sacrifice—so those who believed could spend eternity with Him.

The dam broke. I grabbed her hand and sobbed, "It's okay, Mom. It's okay. We'll be okay." I don't know who I was trying to convince—her or myself. She didn't need my permission, yet I felt the strong urge to tell her that I didn't resent her choice to let go. As a believer in Jesus, I knew she was on her way to the safety and security of heaven.

I could see that God had made her ready. A supernatural peace mixed with the tears in her eyes. It bolstered me into a different kind of readiness. God made me ready for Mom's suffering to end and mine to begin in a whole new way until we meet again in glory. The

Lord supplied each of us our own brand of courage—
hers in the going, mine in the staying.

And it was enough.

CHAPTER 2

HOSPICE

*"You have put me in the lowest pit,
in the darkest depths."*

—Psalm 88:6

As a single parent, Mom lived out her days sacrificing more than I will ever know. She spent hours in prayer for Sarah and me. She signed every card with, "I love you, Always and Forever." And there were many cards. Cards for every occasion and non-occasion. Sarah and I never missed an opportunity to tease her about it. In a speech during Mom's funeral, Sarah joked that Mom singlehandedly kept the greeting card business afloat for decades. Mom sent cards to people for birthdays, holidays, anniversaries, births, deaths, illnesses, celebrations, because she saw you on the street one day, because she heard you liked flowers and she did, too, because there was weather—any kind of weather—because it was Tuesday, or because she had a card sitting on her counter and compulsively had to send it to someone.

She was a mom in the truest sense of the word, always putting her kids before herself, always going above and beyond. The first time Sarah broke her arm in elementary school, Mom stayed up all night to make sure Sarah's arm stayed elevated while she slept, to minimize pain and swelling. She did the same for me when I had my wisdom teeth extracted—setting the microwave timer to beep every four hours through the night so she could change my ice packs.

Then the tables turned.

Suddenly Sarah and I found ourselves in role reversal confusion. Our whole lives, Mom was the one taking care of us—mopping up our stomach flu messes, wiping feverish foreheads, cooking chicken soup. My head reeled with a crisis of identity as I lifted Mom from bed to wheelchair to toilet, terrified I would drop her. I hated seeing her so weak and helpless.

I wanted the Mom I knew.

It was no longer safe for her to live alone, but my sister and I didn't know what to do. We didn't have money or insurance for in-home care, and Sarah had to work. I had three kids to look after and could only stay in Michigan for six weeks before flying back to my established life in Cape Town. Besides, I couldn't meet her extensive medical and physical needs even if I were available.

The only viable option was the Hospice House—a residential facility on the south side of town for those in palliative care. I bristled at the thought of it. Once admitted, patients didn't usually leave. Mom tried to persuade me otherwise, saying it was possible for patients to just stay there for a while to regain their strength, and then go home. Or maybe she was trying to persuade herself. I knew it was wishful thinking, and my stomach turned. But we had no other choice.

We scheduled an appointment with a kind hospice worker who came to Mom's condo. "There's a wait list," she explained. And we couldn't wait. She acknowledged the urgency and suggested that Mom be admitted to the hospital to stall until a room became available. It felt morbid to wish for a room at the Hospice House to open up, because it meant we were wishing for a stranger to die.

Mom's doctor agreed to a hospital admittance. We planned for an ambulance to pick her up from the condo. I was alone with Mom while we waited for the EMTs to arrive. An awkward silence filled the room. "Can I gather up some things you might want to take with you?" I asked, trying to make conversation.

This might be her last day at home. As much as I pushed and shoved at the thought, it kept elbowing its way back into my mind.

Mom wanted to try changing out of her nightgown but discovered she didn't have the strength to do so. Sitting in a borrowed wheelchair, she opted instead to wear her purple velour sweat suit on top of her nightgown. With some difficulty, we managed to get her arms into the zip-up jacket, careful not to disturb the oxygen tubes. Then Mom looked down at the pants. Realizing she'd have to stand up to get them on, she said, "Never mind. I'll just go like this." Coming from a woman who put on lipstick just to drive to an ATM, I knew she was in bad shape.

The EMTs arrived, and the dreaded moment fell heavy on the doorstep. Fear knocked on my heart as they rapped on the door. There was no turning back.

"I'll follow behind the ambulance and meet you at the hospital," I promised through the grief lodged in the back of my throat. She nodded. As one of the paramedics wheeled Mom backward out of her condo, our eyes met. The look on her face was unforgettable. She feigned a smile, a sign of her resolve. Her green eyes begged me to believe everything would be okay—but we both knew it was the last time she would pass through that door.

The silence after she left haunted me. I let myself pause and scan the scene that remained. Suddenly the possessions I had held dear for so long seemed trivial and empty. What did these things matter without Mom's presence?

I slipped out of the stark hospital room and into the sanitized hallway, making the excuse of needing some water. The truth was, I needed far more than a drink. I found the doctor sitting at a desk, dictating orders to be transcribed. I waited patiently, heart pounding in my chest. He turned and looked at me. "Can I help you?"

"Yes, um, I'm sorry to bother you. You just saw my mom in room 504, and I know this isn't a very fair question to ask, but . . . Well, the thing is, my husband is still in South Africa and is planning to arrive in three weeks. When we booked his flight, we didn't realize my mom's condition was so unstable, so . . . Well, um, I know you probably hate this question, and you can't see the future, but if you could give a ballpark estimate as to how long she has left, what would you guess? Or, at least, do you think I should try to get my husband to come sooner?"

"Two weeks," he stated matter-of-factly. "But maybe today, maybe tomorrow."

My heart splatted onto the polished linoleum floor. I smiled politely and nodded my thanks for his prediction.

I couldn't bring myself to tell my sister. I couldn't bring myself to tell anyone. I went back to Mom's room, pasted on a plastic smile, and pretended everything was fine. At least Mom was in good hands now. She was strapped into the hospital bed with guardrails raised on each side so she couldn't fall out. Nurses were on duty around the clock, so she always had a trained professional to help her go to the bathroom. Someone would make sure she took all eighteen of her prescriptions at the appropriate times. I tried to peptalk myself into seeing the perks, but really, everything just looked bleak.

I waited until we got back to Sarah's house before I borrowed her cell phone and dialed the bazillion digits for the international calling card and pin number and country code to talk to Kagiso. Cupping the receiver to my ear, I waited as the invisible line connected me to my husband, half a world away.

"Hello?"

I swallowed hard. "The doctor says two weeks, maximum." Just speaking the words out loud felt like a blow to the chest. "I need you to come."

A long sigh blew into my ear. "I'm sorry. I didn't realize it was this bad." He paused, the weight of the world filling the silence. "I'll see what I can do, but I don't even know if work will let me leave for that long. Besides, changing my plane ticket is going to be expensive. Where's that money going to come from?"

"I don't know where you're going to get the money," I snapped. "I don't care where it comes from or how much it takes. I just need you here. I can't manage the kids on my own with everything falling apart so fast. I can barely manage myself."

Kagiso said he would do his best, but could make no guarantees. We ended the conversation with many questions unanswered.

Before leaving Cape Town, I had made plans for close friends of ours to visit us in Michigan while we were there. Rodger and Linda were dear South African friends who were studying in St. Louis for two years before returning to their home country. Our kids adored one another. Rodger and Linda offered to make the seven-hour drive just so we could spend time together. When we made the arrangements, however, we had no idea how much my mom's health would decline before they arrived.

"Do you still want us to come?" Linda probed over the phone, two days before they were due to make the long trek. "If it's not a good time with so much going on, we understand."

"I don't just *want* you to come—I *need* you."

"Okay," Linda answered. "We'll be there soon."

Sarah and I welcomed them with waves of gratitude, very aware that this providence was directly from God.

Kagiso was still in Cape Town, and Kent had left to lead a youth retreat in Colorado for a week. We'd been on our own with three kids and a dying mother. Rodger, Linda, Linda's mom, and their three children arrived in a packed white minivan and carried us on wings of grace. Sarah and Kent's home accommodated all eleven of us, and I felt every letter of the word *community*. Our kids giggled and played, swapping stories as if no time had passed. They laid blankets on the grass and ate picnic lunches in the backyard. They built a bonfire in the fire pit, roasted marshmallows, and made s'mores, the kids reveling in the sticky messes all over their grinning faces.

Rodger, Linda, and Linda's mom took care of everything from childcare to meal preparation, because "a friend loves at all times"—even when the humid summer air is sticky with dread, and someone you love is about to die (Prov. 17:17).

Mom spent a couple of days in the hospital before we got the news. The Hospice House had an opening. Mom could move in that afternoon. Relief and devastation hit me at the same time. I knew she would receive the best care there, but I wasn't ready to admit that it had come to this. Mom wasn't, either. She wanted a detour, a different road. We all did.

The facility was beautiful, like a fancy hotel or a bed-and-breakfast. But even the lavish adornments couldn't mask what it really was: a holding cell. A waiting room for eternity. The carpeted hallways whispered of the many souls who passed through—one last pit stop before reaching their final destination.

A kind nurse helped Mom settle into an ivory recliner as she gave Mom, Sarah, and me the routine welcome conversation. It was more than I could bear. All three of us hung by a thread, ready to snap under the weight of it all. Mom was beside herself, weeping and repeating, "I don't want to be here. I don't need to be here. This is a mistake. I shouldn't be here."

It broke me. I fled to the bathroom and collapsed on the cold tiles, sobbing violent heaves into the handicapped toilet. I pounded the seat and screamed at God without words. How could He let this happen? I cried and cried until the tears ran dry and my throat flared.

I couldn't bring myself to go back to Sarah's house to face my kids with such a hollow smile and puffy, red eyes. I had nothing left to give, and couldn't handle playing the mom role when all I wanted was to see my own mom live. I couldn't remember ever feeling so empty, so depleted. I shuffled into the sterile, hushed hallway, leaned against the wall, and whispered to Sarah, "I can't. Just call Dad and tell him we need to sleep at his house tonight, and call Rodger and Linda and tell them we'll be home tomorrow. They'll understand. I just can't." I was so spent I couldn't even pick up the phone.

With mustered-up strength and painted-on enthusiasm, Sarah nodded and set about the task at hand. "I'll drive home and get us some pajamas and clothes for tomorrow. You just stay here. I'll come back and pick you up."

I returned to Mom's new room, curled up on the wicker love seat, and covered myself with her purple velour jacket. The air conditioning made the room freezing cold. Mom was sound asleep in the leather recliner, and I was glad. The emotion had run me dry. I fell fast asleep, knees to my chest. Sarah returned an hour later with all the arrangements in place. We promised Mom we would come back the next day and told her to get some rest. It felt so wrong leaving her there. My promise to return held no weight. We didn't even know if she would see tomorrow.

I slumped into the passenger seat of Sarah's silver sedan. The robin's-egg blue of the sky taunted me with its brightness, rubbing in the fact that life goes on even when it doesn't.

Sarah pointed to a cooler at my feet. "There are two spoons inside."

I reached down, opened the plastic container, and found a half gallon of mint chocolate chip ice cream. I breathed out as much of a laugh as I could muster, and we ate in silence as she drove. There were just no words. That might have been the only time in my life when even ice cream failed to make me feel better.

As we walked into Dad's house, he and his wife, Angela, greeted us with smiles of empathy. As a retired doctor and a full-time nurse, they could imagine what we had been through and were wise enough to give us space. We thanked them for hosting us on such short notice, said good night, and went down to the spare bedroom in the basement to sleep. It struck me then that I had never actually slept in this particular house of theirs. They had moved into it after Sarah and I had stopped having our childhood weekends at Dad's, and I'd only ever been to this house for meals or family events. It felt foreign, yet familiar. I felt safe.

The next morning, I was still angry at the sun for shining. Somehow Sarah persuaded me to go for a walk, entirely against my will. I squinted in disgust at the sun and blinked back resentful tears. Everything hurt—my head, my back, my neck, my feet. I had just bought cross-trainers, but my new shoes were still stiff and unforgiving and a nasty blister formed on my heel. Sarah waited patiently while I stopped again and again to loosen the laces and adjust my sock. How could I be complaining about one lousy blister when my mom was dying of cancer? It hurt to walk, but I had to keep going. As with the rest of life, that's the only way I would ever get home.

Through very generous friends, the Lord paved the way for Kagiso to rebook his flight and arrive sooner than planned. Kent got back from Colorado, and Sarah and I both breathed more easily, despite the stress that still hung overhead.

After Mom stopped the chemo, she actually started to feel better. It was no small providence that we were in the States during this brief window. Mom got to do things with the kids that she might not have been able to do otherwise. We loaded Mom, her spare oxygen tanks, and the hospice wheelchair into the car and visited my grandma in her nursing home, laughing and reminiscing over slices of cherry pie. We made memories out of hobo pies over an open fire, sticky ice-cream chins, and Fourth of July sparklers in the driveway. Summer tasted like sandy s'mores, just as it should. God etched precious memories into impressionable minds, I snapped photos in abundance, and we milked each moment dry.

The kids took turns climbing into Grandma's hospice bed, curling up close, not noticing how swollen her abdomen had become from excess, cancerous fluid. They colored with her and read for her, and sometimes just watched Curious George DVDs, leaving trails of pretzel crumbs on the white sheets. Oblivious to the brevity of life. We helped Mom from the recliner to her wheelchair, unhooked the oxygen from the room wall and attached the tubes to a portable tank, then wheeled her out to the sitting area to eat ice cream and draw pictures. Sometimes we'd go to the children's playroom down the hall. The kids took turns riding the rocking horse, doing puzzles, and asking Grandma to read to them. She gazed at them with all the delight in the world, capturing each moment as a still frame in her mind.

Mom had a constant flow of visitors—relatives, church friends, coworkers from her teaching years, even old school friends she hadn't seen for ages. Their presence was a visible testimony of the impact she'd had on countless lives over the years. Yet the fact that so many made an effort to stop by told me that they, too, realized she was on her last lap. Not a day went by when there weren't a handful of people coming to check on her and bring her gifts, treats, and cards. Her room filled up with flowers, handwritten notes, and plates of homemade baked goods. She insisted on showering and getting dressed and out of bed every day, no matter how she felt.

One sunny afternoon, we arrived at the Hospice House for a visit, my kids skipping enthusiastically through the halls. I followed, rounding a corner only to be faced with a stretcher parked along the wall, a white sheet covering a lifeless body. Instinctively, I averted my eyes and covered my mouth to keep from gagging. Even with the stark contrast of exuberant life galloping down the passageway, there was no hiding the purpose of this place. I felt it in my stomach every time I crossed the threshold of the front door. My nostrils proclaimed the truth with every breath—I could smell it in the air. I wondered what it felt like to be a patient and not a visitor, sitting with feet dangling over the edge of eternity.

As much as we tried to make the most of every moment, the moments were numbered. And they were running out.

One Friday evening, I escorted Mom out of the Hospice House to attend a friend's wedding, the summer breeze warm on our cheeks. We verbally ticked the checklist before leaving her room, making sure we had extra tanks of portable oxygen and plenty of spare batteries. We crammed pills and a bottle of water into her overstuffed purse before I pushed her wheelchair to the car waiting in the parking lot. By the time I managed to slip behind the steering wheel, I was sweating. But Mom was happy, and that was all that mattered.

At the church, I did my best to blink back tears as friends asked to pose with Mom for photographs. *These will be the last pictures they have together,* I thought. At the reception, people who knew Mom looked at me with sympathetic eyes, saying without words what we all knew to be true: this would be the last wedding Mom would attend on earth, before the great wedding banquet of the Lamb.

Mom smiled and laughed from her static position at the table, listening to wedding speeches and watching the bride and groom sway in their first dance together as husband and wife. She didn't seem to mind that I had to get food for her from the buffet, or that she had to drink water incessantly because of the side effects of her medication. I doled out pain pills at the appropriate times, and all was going well until she needed to use the bathroom. Maneuvering a wheelchair through a wedding reception hall crowded with round tables and even more people proved no small task—but it was nothing compared to trying to push the wheelchair into the non-handicapped bathroom stall. I got pinned between the stall door and the chair before realizing that both of us and the wheelchair weren't going to fit inside with the door closed. I pried myself out of the bind, showed Mom where to position her arms for the best support, and prayed that she wouldn't fall. All we could do was laugh at the hilarity of the scene.

Back at the Hospice House, we laughed some more. Like rebellious teenagers, we arrived at the residence after curfew, when the doors were already locked. We pressed the intercom and waited outside for the on-call nurse to buzz us in. When we heard the buzzer, I quickly hit the handicapped button to activate the automatic doors.

Trying to hurry through before the doors closed, I didn't notice the raised lip of the doorframe on the ground. The wheelchair lurched to a stop. My stomach plunged into the back of the chair as Mom's head jerked forward in near whiplash. I apologized profusely through hysterical laughter, doing my best to lift the chair over the bump and through the doorway. I wasn't fast enough. The automatic door slammed closed on my left bicep, leaving an immediate bruise. I fought my way through the narrowing gap and proved victorious. It's hard to be quiet when you're laughing uncontrollably—an irony not lost on Mom or me, as we muffled our giggles in a sleepy building where death reigned.

In the days that followed, I didn't want the mark on my arm to fade. It told a story. I wanted to keep the bruise forever, a living testimony to the memory and the moment. Maybe I just wanted time to stand still. But the days forged on. I watched the bruise morph from black to purple to greenish blue. My story, and my bruise, were fading—and so was my mom.

After nearly six weeks in Michigan, my thirtieth birthday landed just four days before Kagiso, the kids, and I were due to fly back to Cape Town. I dreaded it—not because I cared at all about turning thirty, but because I knew it would be my last birthday with my mom. More than that, we were about to leave her for good. When my birthday arrived, we ordered Chicken Pad Thai from Thai

Palace and took it to the Hospice House. Eating together in the common sitting room, the kids bustled with excitement over my birthday. I tried to keep them quiet, but how could they understand that people were dying in all those rooms with open doors? The kids were full of life and unable to contain it, and I felt awful for trying to make them.

That evening we had an extended family gathering at Sarah's house with my uncles, aunts, and cousins. Mom was there with her wheelchair and a radiant smile. She gave me a gold and silver watch—her last of a million material gifts to me in my lifetime. And I just kept swallowing down thick lumps in my throat and blinking back tears, knowing we held less than a handful of days in her presence.

The day before we left, Mom made one last request. She wanted to go to Captain Sundae, our favorite local ice-cream spot. I remember balking on the inside. We were making an international trip the next day, I was trying to pack up six weeks' worth of living for five people, and it was such a nuisance to drive all the way to the Hospice House and get her and her wheelchair and pills and oxygen and batteries and water and purse and everything else loaded into the car, then unloaded, then loaded back again. In my selfishness, I didn't feel like granting this dying woman the simple pleasure of one last Tommy Turtle sundae. I didn't want to endure the pain of one more "last" thing.

But we did it anyway. Sarah and Kent came, too, and my kids talked about it for months afterward. Mom relished the moment. She sat in her wheelchair with a big grin on her face, drinking in the sun and smiles on the kids' faces. Savoring each minute and bite of pecans and whipped cream. When you notice that you're getting to the last of the presents under the tree, you start to unwrap the gifts more slowly and deliberately, careful not to tear any piece of the paper-thin moment.

The day of departure arrived. The bags stood packed, passports ready. All we had to do was say good-bye.

All we had to do.

My feet felt heavy walking down the Hospice House corridor. As we stood in the familiar room for the last time, Kagiso asked my mom to pray over each of our kids. His request blindsided me. Mom sat in her wheelchair and prayed through heavy sobs, wads of wet tissues gripped tight in her shaking fists. I stood by the bedside at least four feet away, blinking profusely. Fidgeting with the duvet and tapping my foot in a vain attempt to get through the moment. I knew I should be memorizing her every word, engraving her prayers into the treasure box of my heart, but I couldn't do it. It was too much to bear.

We gave our last tearful hugs and walked out of the room, leaving her behind. Thirty years of unbridled love for my mom twisted tight around my esophagus, and I choked on my own grief. My six-year-old daughter let out a sudden, howling wail. Kagiso scooped her up as I pushed my way into a bathroom stall and vomited. Acid residue from the fall of humankind. I flushed the pieces of my shattered heart and shuffled out of the building, emptier than ever before.

CHAPTER 3

DIVORCE

"I will not leave you or forsake you."

—Joshua 1:5 ESV

September 1988

Sarah says we were playing Super Mario Brothers on Nintendo when they came into the living room, but I just remember the couch. My parents sat on opposite ends of the three-seater sofa, an empty cushion between them, while Sarah and I took turns shifting back and forth from one lap to the other. A perfect glimpse into the pattern that would become our lives.

It was the first time I had heard that word, and I didn't understand it: *Divorce.*

At the tender age of seven, I watched the trophy of home fall from its glass-encased pedestal and shatter on unforgiving earth. Until then, I lived in spoiled ignorance of the world at large, protected by a gorgeous, three-thousand-square-foot home on Lake Michigan. I thought every kid lived with a mom, a dad, and a happily ever after.

Dad did the talking; Mom just cried. It was obvious that this was a one-sided decision. Until a few weeks before that evening, Mom was clueless about Dad's change of heart. She was as blindsided by his announcement as Sarah and me. Mom dug in her heels, but the foundation beneath her feet gave way, and she shed her dreams along with her tears. I took her cue and let the tears fall, too, hot and slow down my cheeks, still oblivious to the actual implications of that somber night.

A few days later, my mind flashed back to an afternoon when my dad stood at the desk next to the kitchen, landline phone cupped to his ear. I overheard words I wasn't supposed to hear. Words of affection to someone who was not my mom. I couldn't reconcile the words at the time, so I pushed them away. Now they rushed back, demanding attention. Demanding action. I determined to find out who the other woman was. Not wanting Sarah to be hurt, my friend Mandy and I paced the elementary school playground at recess. Her beach-blonde hair bobbed up and down as we marched back and forth, brainstorming names and faces. Eventually I settled on one particular woman at the hospital nurses' station, where my cardiologist dad made his rounds. *Audrey*. Yes, it had to be her. She was way too nice to me.

I vowed that I would make her life miserable until she decided it wouldn't be worth it to break up a family and backed away. Forever. I hadn't yet seen the movie *The Parent Trap*, but it was the same theory. I had a grand plan to reunite my parents. This would not be how my story ended.

I didn't trust God to make the broken things whole. I had to do it myself.

One day, not long after the Nintendo interruption, Mom whisked Sarah and me off for a weekend away. When we got back, Dad was gone. The next afternoon, when I came home from school, he was still gone. And the day after that. And the day after that. Every morning that followed, for months, when Mom dropped me off in my second grade classroom, I went straight to the coat closet, tucked myself inside, and cried. Terrified that one day I would get home from school, and, like my dad, Mom would be gone too.

From then on, Sarah and I were sent back and forth like Ping-Pong balls across a table-tennis net, bouncing from one parent to the other. We landed with a brief click on the table before being gently tapped back to the other side. Sometimes Mom scored a point, and sometimes Dad did, but in table tennis, the ball never wins. It just gets dents.

One Friday evening, while visiting Dad at his first rental cottage after he moved out, my seven-year-old mind wondered aloud, "Who cooks for you?"

"I do it myself," he answered, pride painted across his face. The expression vanished as soon as the smoke detector went off—a piercing shriek at painful decibels. It was funny at first, but soon grew irritating, blaring every half hour until Dad finally climbed up and removed the batteries.

I don't remember the bedrooms in that cottage. I just remember going for walks in the neighborhood and stopping to greet a family friend who lived down the street. He smiled as we talked, but I saw the pity in his eyes. He knew why we were there.

Dad didn't last long in that first neighborhood— a few months, maybe. Then he moved to an apartment complex on the other side of town, about twenty minutes away. Dad let Sarah and me fold down the back seats of his parked vehicle so we could play office in the garage. He let us help him wash the car on Saturday mornings before we went to play tennis at a nearby court. I celebrated my eighth birthday twice—once at home with Mom, and again at Dad's new apartment. Dad made a sign with markers on computer paper and taped it to his dining room wall: "Kate the Great is Eight!" I got two cakes and two sets of presents. Maybe having divorced parents wasn't so bad after all.

Soon after Dad moved to the apartment complex, Sarah and I met Angela. One Saturday evening, Dad told us we were going out for dinner. This was typical of a weekend at his house, so I didn't think anything of it— until he said a "friend" would be joining us. My stomach knotted. I knew this "friend" was the one I had heard Dad talking to on the phone before the divorce announcement. In my mind at the time, she was the reason my home fell apart.

From the first meeting, I heaved all the blame for my parents' divorce onto Angela's shoulders. I didn't care if it was fair or reasonable. I knew the divorce wasn't Mom's idea. I still loved my dad and didn't want to hate him—so I hated Angela instead. I never even gave her a chance. I set my jaw in a permanent scowl whenever she was around. In conversation, I purposely avoided eye contact with her. I kept my words to a minimum. I acted like a real brat. I reasoned that if I could make her life unpleasant enough, she would get sick of the cruel treatment and push off. Then my dad would realize his folly in leaving my mom, and we could go back to living our happily ever after.

But that first dinner out with Angela turned into a regular fixture during Dad's weekends. Angela started showing up for dinner at Dad's apartment when we were there. Whenever my "mean game" slipped, I quickly swerved it back on track. After the divorce was final just over a year later, Dad announced that he and Angela were moving in together. They were buying a new house on the same side of town, still about twenty minutes from Mom's.

My plan was failing. Instead of going to "Dad's house," we would be going to "Dad and Angela's house." The addition of those two words fueled my animosity. I stepped it up a notch and launched a campaign to get Sarah to join my endeavors. I begged and pleaded with her to be mean, too, but she wasn't persuaded. She appeared to be occupied by the personal television Dad and Angela let her have in her new room and the zigzag purple-and-teal paint with underwater wallpaper border they let her choose by herself. Since I didn't have Sarah to back me up, I made sure Angela saw my irritation in everything she did, from how much cream cheese she spread on her bagel in the morning, to the gaudy eggplant color she painted the front door.

Though my dad moved from one temporary accommodation to another, he remained nearby and very involved. He withdrew his daily presence but not his love or his care. He taught us how to play tennis, how to ski, and how to play golf. He made us Belgian waffles every other Saturday morning, with Smucker's boysenberry syrup for me and blueberry for Sarah. Sarah and I spent our weekends at his house shooting hoops in the driveway and watching *Full House* on Friday nights. We played *Mavis Beacon Teaches Typing* and *Where in the World Is Carmen Sandiego?* on the huge desktop computer in the basement until Dad called us for dinner by yodeling a long and playful, "Sooouuup's ooo-oonnn!"

Dad drove with us in the back seat of his burgundy Toyota Previa, making the half hour trek to church every other Sunday, where he dropped us off in the parking lot and drove away. Serve, volley, repeat.

Until the divorce, Mom was able to be a stay-at-home mom. Then Dad stopped making house payments. Mom panicked. She had started working straight out of high school and didn't have a college degree. Her work experience had a gaping hole spanning seven years. Mom stretched herself out before God in prayer, and He stretched out His hand with a precious gift—a job as a reading paraprofessional in an elementary school. It was perfect—Mom loved books and children, and the teaching position gave her the same working hours that Sarah and I were in school. Among five paraprofessionals hired at the same time, Mom was the only one without a college degree. God showed mercy.

Even with the job, however, Mom couldn't manage the house payments. Less than a year after Dad left, Mom, Sarah, and I had no choice but to move out of the blue beach house that had welcomed me home as a newborn one hot week in early August, eight years earlier. The house that had hidden Easter eggs in every nook and cranny, high and low, while Sarah and I ran around in our pajamas, clutching baskets and letting out squeals. The house where I had bunk beds that pressed against kite wallpaper, and instead of counting sheep, I counted kites until I fell asleep each night, except when I begged to sleep in Sarah's room. On those evenings, I climbed into her double canopy bed, and Mom sandwiched between our two blonde heads, one resting on each shoulder of her velour pajama gown. She stayed for a while and read to us, book after glorious book. Her voice rose and fell like gentle waves rolling over each page, and words became my lullaby.

But that house is a memory now, and after looking and looking, Mom caved in desperation and settled for an old pump house that had been renovated into a five-hundred-square-foot, two-bedroom cottage. It stood on the same street as the blue house, just a mile south—near enough that we didn't have to switch schools, but so close that we drove past our old house almost every day.

The big blue house taunted me with its nearness—
a stone's throw from the road, and yet completely out of
reach. A daily reminder of what used to be. Of what had
been so abruptly snatched away.

The tan pump house stood less than a car's length
from the road. We couldn't even park our car in front
of the tiny cottage. When trucks or snowplows passed
by, the glasses in our kitchen cupboards rattled. One
night just before we moved in, Sarah and I lay on the
empty floor of the cottage living room, the ugly, brown-
striped carpet our only source of entertainment while
Mom painted her bedroom. Mom's tears of exhaustion
and frustration spilled through the thin walls. My eyes
met Sarah's, and my heart bled.

Mom vowed the rental would only be for six months
while she got back on her feet. But as a newly employed,
single mother of two, she always fell a step behind, and
those six months turned into a year, and then two, and
then ten. The thrill of sharing a room grew stale, and with
furniture from two bedrooms packed into one, eventually
Sarah and I had to turn our preteen torsos sideways so
we could shimmy between the white frame of the bunk
beds and the matching wardrobe to reach the overflow-
ing excuse of a closet. Instead of drifting off to *Goodnight
Moon* or *Polar Express*, we argued and bickered, "I want
the door open," "Well, I want it closed," and "I want the
radio on," "Too bad, I want it off."

The significant downsizing meant that most of our
belongings remained stacked high in cardboard boxes
and Rubbermaid totes in the pump-house garage. A single path remained clear—just wide enough for one person

at a time to walk through from the driveway into the house. If visitors wanted us to know they'd arrived, they had to walk around the back of the cottage and through the enclosed area where our basset hound, Lucy, peed and pooped. In ten years, we never unpacked the boxes or cleared the garage. We lived on the edge of hope, persuaded that maybe tomorrow we'd find a better place to land.

At one point, Mom decided to re-wallpaper the wall that led from the bedrooms and bathroom through the kitchen to the living room. She chose a happy floral print to replace the drab burgundy-and-tan stripes. Mom considered slapping the new wallpaper over the old, but decided to do it the right way and peel off the stripes first. Sarah and I armed ourselves with scrapers to speed up the work. We scraped and scraped, until we found another layer of wallpaper under the stripes. Mom groaned. We scraped some more. A third layer revealed itself. We pushed our arm muscles to the limit as not three, not four, but *eleven* layers of wallpaper appeared under the burgundy and tan. All we could do was laugh in disbelief. When we reached the bare wall, we found stenciled Dutch girls and boys staring at us through faded tulips.

On another occasion, ants infested our bathroom—huge, black, carpenter ants that crunched when we squished them. No matter how many we killed, more appeared. Finally, Mom had had enough. She asked the landlord to call an exterminator. The pest control worker arrived decked in brown overalls to assess the situation. The next thing we knew, he was tearing up the cracked linoleum floor in our bathroom. We peered inside as he finished—every square inch of the surface teemed with ants. We couldn't see a single hint of wood beneath— just swirls of busy black movement. I had bad dreams for weeks.

All of this took place back in the untouched era of middle-class American suburbia when divorce had not yet become the norm. When I was the only kid I knew in my grade whose parents were no longer married. It wouldn't be until fifth grade that I learned of a fellow classmate whose mom and dad had separated. With mutual sympathy, we formed a fast, unspoken bond, the commonality of divorce the strand that braided us together. He understood. Others tried, but unless they had experienced the physical tearing apart, they could never fully relate.

When people heard my parents were divorced, I became known as one of those kids from a "broken home." The label irked me; it wasn't even my fault. I felt pitied and hated it. It would be years before I realized that all human beings are living in a broken home. The whole world is broken, and still crumbling. Ever since Eve bit the fruit in the Garden of Eden, God's people have been straining for wholeness. Longing to belong. The tension pulled within me. Even before I could name its source, my body joined the universal strain for home.

And so, my childhood definition of home was formed with puzzle pieces from two different boxes. None of them matched or fit very well, but that was all I had to use. Far different and perhaps more tumultuous from that of my closest friends, whose parents were still together. Their puzzle pieces joined smooth and flush. Yet a sense of security at mom's house remained, untouched. Sure, there was the bimonthly packing of weekend suitcases and most of my friends didn't own two toothbrushes in two different houses, but we were well cared for, and the Lord provided.

I was always the homebody, my sister, the independent. My dad loved to tell the story of how Sarah declared at age three that she was ready for her own apartment. On the weekends when Dad shuttled us over to his house, I got homesick for my mom, even though Sarah and I were only there for two nights at a time. Mom sought to ease the sting with a bandage of her own making. First she bought a scrap of velour fabric, just like the material of the gown she wore each night, the one my arm brushed against as she read to us in bed. Then she even recorded audio cassette tapes of herself reading aloud some of our favorite books and slipped them into our overnight bags. Every second weekend, I lay in bed at Dad's, clutching the square of gray velour. I closed my eyes, listened to the tape player, and pretended she was there, reading me to sleep.

CHAPTER 4

STUCK

*"Save me, O God, for the waters have come up
to my neck. I sink in the miry depths, where there
is no foothold. I have come into the deep waters;
the floods engulf me. I am worn out calling for help;
my throat is parched. My eyes fail,
looking for my God."*

—Psalm 69:1–3

The childhood years that followed the shattering divorce announcement were emotionally draining. Wearing two hats exhausted me. I flipped back and forth between being the doctor's kid, who roamed on a long leash and downhill skied the Rockies once a year, and the single mama's girl, the conscientious people pleaser who could see her mom was struggling. Tension loomed thick every time Mom and Dad saw each other. Dad planted negative comments about Mom in my ear, and Mom chipped in her own venom-filled attacks toward Dad.

When the divide tossed me in two different directions, my church anchored me. Mom never failed to take us to church, on Sundays for Sunday school and services and Wednesdays for youth group. My maternal grandma, the only biological grandparent still living by the time I was born, babysat every Thursday night so Mom could go to prayer meeting at church. I can still see Mom's handwriting in my mind's eye—every week she scrawled "SIP 7pm" in the Thursday box on her calendar, and I knew she was planning to go to Servants in Prayer. This single weekly commitment spoke volumes about Mom's high priority for prayer. Grandma read to us and played the Peter Rabbit board game and Pigs in the Pen, and as the years passed, she taught us to play Kings in the Corner. Every Thursday night I complained that I couldn't fall asleep, and she told me it was because I still had my socks on. I believed her. And she was right.

Those were Thursdays, but Sundays and Wednesdays, we were at church. And I found God there. Or rather, that's where He opened my eyes to see Him.

Church, and especially youth group, became a nest to me, as I faltered and flailed in my weak attempts to learn to fly. Each time I went back, wings battered and body worn from the beating of wind and rain, it sheltered me. The people within her walls became my family. They stood by my side in quiet support while I grieved the dissolution of my parents' marriage. The church caught my tears and they held me, and they held me, and they held me some more as I tried in vain to splint the injured bones of our fractured home.

Church fed me. Spiritually, yes—but physically too. With cash left anonymously in unmarked envelopes at just the right time, with frozen turkeys and hams on our doorstep every Thanksgiving and Christmas, they fed us. Mom opened the attached note to find grocery money tucked inside, and wiped away salty tears of gratitude along with her pride. When she had used up all her sick days and personal days at work, various women from church let me crash on their couch while I had the stomach flu. They poured me cups of 7-Up and left empty wastebaskets by my side so I could throw up while watching *The Price Is Right*. Time after time, God showed up when I had a need.

Throughout my elementary years, I enjoyed school. I had a core group of friends, and we moved together from grade to grade. There was stability—even a hominess about our little school community. Everyone knew each other, and I knew what to expect.

Then came sixth grade.

Sixth grade was the worst school year of my educational career. It was the first year of middle school, which, in my school district, meant that eight elementary schools fed into one building. The building was, however, divided into two segments—East Side and West Side. And wouldn't you know . . . *all* my friends from elementary got assigned to West Side, and I got stuck on East. Alone.

I was lost, and I hated it. I wanted to go back to comfort and familiarity. I wanted the security I'd sensed through fifth grade. Instead, I had to fend for myself, find my own way, forge new bonds. We were assigned to one homeroom teacher, and then we'd move with the same students to different teachers and subjects every hour. I'd never had a teacher I didn't like. *Until then.* My homeroom teacher was beyond strict. Her strictness came across as harshness, and she terrified me. To get an A in her class, she required us to read for an hour every single night. As an adult I would pay for that luxury, but as an eleven-year-old with homework from six other classes, an hour of mandatory reading seemed unattainable and unfair. I resented my teacher for enforcing such rules and snatching away my joy.

Then came the worst news of all: we all had to go to sixth grade camp for a week. Could there be anything worse? An insecure mama's girl, I was perfectly content to stay home with my mom in the house that I knew and not sleep anywhere else for the rest of my life. New situations and unfamiliar routines rattled me. It was so early in the school year, I didn't even have any friends yet. Surely there was some way I could get out of it. Maybe fake a fever? Sprain my ankle? I found no loopholes; attendance was required. I felt sick to my stomach at the thought of being away from my mom for a whole week with people I didn't know, in a place I'd never been. But I went, hoping I could just mind my own business and play wallflower.

It was worse than expected.

The entire week was packed with awkward icebreakers and team-building activities, like a ropes course, scavenger hunt, and survival skills test—probably a blast for the outgoing kids; a nightmare for me. The team-building activities were designed to make people uncomfortable—presumably to force us to depend on one another and recognize our need to work together. I was miserable.

I cried. A lot. I begged to go home. The leaders wouldn't let me. Camp was mandatory; no exceptions. I cried some more. Still they refused.

Even though my teachers wouldn't let me go home, they did offer a compromise: they allowed my mom to come to the campsite for a night. So my selfless mother drove to the campgrounds after work one day and slept on the floor of the cabin, amidst a slew of bunk beds and smelly sixth graders. She woke up before the sun the next morning and drove the long distance home to be at work in time. She couldn't grant me my heart's desire to go home, but she could grant me the gift of her presence. And that night, that was enough.

God might not have let me go home when I wanted to—but He did send His Spirit, present in my mom, to lie on the floor next to my bunk bed in the darkest of nights. Though the Lord doesn't always answer my prayers the way I want, He *always* grants the gift of His presence.

Little did I know how much I would need it in the years to come.

With time, sixth grade got a little better. I gradually adjusted to having multiple teachers and switching classrooms every hour. I even made a friend. A best friend. Though we've drifted apart as the years have passed, Andrea was exactly what I needed in that season of change and awkwardness. We both agreed that the "one hour of reading every night" was a ridiculous rule. We laughed about the same things. She was funny and carefree and helped me loosen up about my new, undesirable environment.

Our moms even worked together at the same elementary school—the one just across the football field from our middle school. Every day after school, we loaded up our backpacks and trudged side by side across the field to wait in the teachers' lounge, eating snacks until our moms finished work.

One snowy night that winter, something woke me up, and I couldn't fall back to sleep. I shuffled to the living room to find my mom sitting at the table with the lamp on, shoulders hunched. Her palms held her face, and when she looked up at me, I saw red, swollen eyes. A wet tissue fell from her shaking hand. I sat on the arm of the blue leather couch to steady myself, unable to step any farther into the room.

Then she told me. Andrea's mom was dead. Her car hit a patch of black ice and slid through an intersection, headlong into a tree.

I couldn't swallow, couldn't speak. At first, I couldn't even cry. For the first time, someone I knew just disappeared into the realm of death, and I didn't know what to do with myself. Grief was an unknown animal; I had no idea how it behaved, or what it would do to me. Like my parents' divorce, I could do nothing. Even though my dad was still alive, I couldn't bring him back. Now Andrea's mom was gone too—forever.

Days later, I went to the funeral home for the visitation. The casket was open. I'd never seen a dead body before. Nothing could've prepared me. Peering into the casket, I was met by a chalk-white complexion and bright coral lipstick—completely uncharacteristic of the warm smile I had come to know every day in the teachers' lounge after school. In that moment I came face-to-face with the brevity of life.

By high school, I'd watched the lives of many others vanish—some old, some young. All unexpected. The shock was the same every time. Even though I'd learned that life is fragile, I hadn't danced with the idea of my own light being snuffed out. Then during spring break of my sophomore year, I went white-water rafting with my dad, Angela, and Sarah.

The setting was the Kern River of Southern California, Class III/IV white-water rapids. For the record, white-water rafting was not my idea. I tagged along because that was The Plan. I did my best to act as adventurous and daring as possible, keeping my lips sealed to make sure they weren't visibly quavering. We stood in a semicircle around our designated raft, all decked out in bathing suits, bright orange life vests, and sky-blue helmets.

As part of his "safety speech" before we got in the raft, our guide read portions of the release form that my dad had signed on my behalf, since I was a minor. "This release essentially states that I know I am going on a white-water rafting trip in a wilderness environment—not on an amusement park ride or to an air-conditioned shopping mall. As a result of the inherent risks in this activity, I know I may die, get hurt, or damage my belongings." At the word *die*, my breath caught in my throat. The guide read on: "I hereby acknowledge that I have voluntarily chosen to go on this white-water rafting trip. Certain risks are inherent in any recreational activity and cannot be eliminated, altered, or controlled, and these risks that contribute to the unique character of the activity can also be the cause of injury, illness, death, and damages." There it was again: *death*. I glanced at my family members standing in a circle next to me. They seemed fine. Nobody looked nervous. *Deep breaths*, I thought. *You can do this. The guide has to read those words to protect the rafting company. It's just standard procedure. Nothing bad is going to happen.*

The guide continued: "Okay, now for some practical rafting rules. Number one: stay in the boat! If you fail to follow the number one rule, at least follow rule number two: don't panic! If you end up in the water, just look for your raft. If it's within reach, swim to it. If not, look for another raft nearby. If no raft is within a short swimming distance, swim to shore. It's as simple as that. Don't panic; just swim!"

On the river, well, I basically held on for dear life as we weaved through protruding boulders. The nose of the raft dove down in despair and lurched up in redemption as I begged, "Please, Lord, let me stay in the boat."

God chose not to answer that prayer. Correction: He *did* answer that prayer, the answer was just "No."

There were six of us in the raft, plus our guide, and Sarah was the only one in the lot with any common sense. The only one brave enough to get out. It went something like this:

Guide: "So, who wants to go back and surf that hole?"

Dad: "Who wants to *what*?"

Guide: "Surf the hole. Basically, we turn the raft around, paddle like crazy upstream until we hit that hole in the rapids where it's swirling downward into a tight spiral, and if we hit it just right, we'll sort of float on top of it for a while without moving anywhere. We might not get it right the first time; it's a pretty tricky maneuver. But it's fine—if we don't manage to surf it on the first try, we can keep going back until we get it right."

Wavering nods and shrugged shoulders indicated an almost unanimous consensus. "No, thanks. I don't want to," Sarah stated boldly.

"Okay, that's cool," said the guide, nonchalantly. "We'll just drop you off on the shore over there and pick you up afterward." I didn't foresee any danger. The way the guide described it, the decision to "surf the hole" (or attempt to do so) just sounded like an extra workout for our biceps.

We paddled over to a little inlet, and Sarah jumped out. The remaining five of us headed for the hole, guide perched on the high tail of the raft. Paddling against the rapids was much more strenuous than trying to direct the raft downstream. "Dig!" the guide shouted. "Harder! Come on, dig!" We lunged and pulled, lunged and pulled, until the swirling hole in the rapids was within reach.

My dad sat directly opposite me. The next thing I remember was seeing his full, six-foot frame lunging toward me, hurtling me backward off the raft's edge into the raging river. I plunged downward before my life jacket raised me up toward the surface. But instead of finding oxygen, my helmet bumped against something hard at the top.

The raft.

All the safety precautions announced at the beginning of the trip went rushing downstream with the current. The guide had given instructions on what to do if the raft was in sight, but he hadn't mentioned anything about being trapped *under it*! I swam to the left. *Raft.* I swam to the right. *More raft.* I felt around in every direction and couldn't find an escape route. Seconds ticked by. I saw no hope in the blurry nightmare.

Well, this is it, I thought. *I've always wondered how I was going to die, and now I have my answer.* The word *death* from the release form rang in my ears. At least I'd had fifteen good years.

Oddly enough, suddenly I felt a calmness. A peace, as if it would be okay if I did die in that moment. The feeling contradicted the anxiety I had known standing on shore less than an hour earlier. On land, I took deep breaths to calm my nerves. Underwater, I didn't have that option— yet panic did not overtake me. Instead, I possessed an odd surety. I was confident that if I did die, there was nothing left undone. I wouldn't have any outstanding debts or unfulfilled regrets if that were to be my end, this side of the curtain.

I'm sure the water was cold, but all I could feel were the burning pleas for air knocking on my rib cage. With open eyes searching the cloudy water, suddenly I felt as if I had taken a deep breath. As if my lungs had been refilled. I calculated the bubbles I could afford to exhale, not wanting my fresh reserve to be depleted. My wits returned and I realized I had to stop floundering, pick a direction, and just swim. I gripped the bottom of the raft, hurled myself to the left, and found air.

"*There you are!*" was the first exclamation I heard before the guide grabbed the shoulders of my life jacket and flung me into the bottom of the raft. I lay there, heaving, gasping. Convulsing. *Glad to be alive.*

Sarah, the only wise land-stander, was on the shore sobbing. She was convinced that she would have to tell Mom that I had drowned in the Kern River. Afterward, she kept repeating, "You were gone for a *long time!*" Even the guide was surprised to see me. He later confessed that he was *this close* to jumping into the rapids to look for me—and apparently guides *never* do that.

In hindsight, the peace I felt remains inexplicable. It had to have been supernatural. It welled up within me from a source wholly other than myself, filled my suffocating lungs with new wind, and carried me to the surface. I wondered if that was how heaven felt. Like a second chance. Like new birth.

Being trapped underwater was the closest I'd ever come to dying. Yet there was peace. Not just any peace, but "the peace of God, which transcends all understanding" (Phil. 4:7). It guarded my heart and mind and showed me that yes, I would be ready when God called me home.

Before going rafting that day, I hadn't thought much about my own death. Even though I had attended funerals, I didn't think it would happen to me. At least, not so soon. I had accepted Christ as my Savior and trusted in His death and resurrection for my eternal destination—but until then, my faith had never been tested to such an extreme measure. That near-death experience was the first time I came face-to-face with the question of whether I was ready. Whether I had confidence in Christ. Whether my hope really was "an anchor for the soul, firm and secure" (Heb. 6:19).

That harrowing experience taught me to be more fully aware that this home on earth is only temporary. It could be snatched away at any moment. We must be ready. I once heard the account of a woman whose husband died in the hospital emergency room. Following the tragedy, she said, "The hospital is no place to sort out your theology. It has to be in place before the emergency strikes."

God used the rafting experience to confirm in my own heart that I'm ready when He calls me home. Blessed assurance, Jesus is mine. It was an anchor of hope that I would cling to much later.

CHAPTER 5

GROWTH

"Better is one day in your courts than a thousand elsewhere; I would rather be a doorkeeper in the house of my God than dwell in the tents of the wicked."

—Psalm 84:10

During my sophomore year of high school, our landlord decided to sell the property where we were living. While we had always wanted a different place, Mom didn't have the means for anything else. Stress levels ran high as Mom searched and searched for a different rental with comparable monthly payments. Nothing existed in our price range. Then Mom announced that our sweet grandma had chipped in to help us secure a loan to buy a house. Our very own house.

Mom found a modest, three-bedroom ranch not far from the big blue house where I was born. We would have more than double the space we had in the roadside pump house. It felt too good to be true. At fifteen, I would have my own bedroom again, and there was even a finished basement. We would have a front door, a two-stall garage, and a separate room for our dining table. Mom was thrilled. To own a home again did wonders for her countenance. A new confidence came with the title "homeowner." She walked with her shoulders back, chin up. We moved in the summer before my junior year of high school with no shortage of help from church friends and family.

And in no time at all, it felt like home.

When I turned sixteen, my dad surprised me with a burgundy '89 Honda Accord with flip-up headlights. "You're an adult now," Dad announced. "You're on your own." I celebrated my newfound freedom by cruising down Lakeshore Drive with Sarah, belting out Will Smith songs with one hand on the steering wheel, the other catching wind through the open sunroof.

In high school, I continued to ping-pong back and forth between identities, searching for a place to land. Dad's lax rules and long leash allowed me to wander into territory Mom would have restricted. I was the goody-goody academic around church friends and at Mom's house, but danced with rebellion among sports friends and at Dad's.

As a freshman, Wednesday nights sounded like praise songs at youth group while Saturday nights tasted like shots of Captain Morgan chased by swigs of warm Coke in a friend's moonlit driveway. The drinking wasn't a regular habit, but the few occasions felt empowering. As if I had gotten away with something and nobody else would ever know. But the exhilaration didn't last long. I plummeted fast into regret. I feared my church friends would learn I was a fraud. Worse, what if my mom found out? Dad wouldn't have cared, but Mom would've been devastated.

Various boys came over to watch movies in Dad's furnished basement. I flitted from one fling to the next with the exception of one longer-term boyfriend. My circle of friends included the ones nominated for homecoming court and prom king and queen—pretty and popular. I tiptoed in their shadows—part of the group, but largely unnoticed. I was craving something, but didn't know what. Maybe I just longed to belong.

Deep down, I knew my double lifestyle was a gross hypocrisy. My commitment to Christ ebbed and flowed. I'm quite certain there were days and even years in high school when people who knew me would have been surprised to learn I called myself a Christian. Like being stretched between Dad's house and Mom's, my heart was divided.

Even into my teenage years, I let my parents' divorce define me. From my middle-class suburban perspective, I only saw peers who had big, beautiful houses, two parents who still loved each other, and plenty of money for lavish family vacations. Peers with their own bedrooms and moms who didn't have to work. I suffered from a severe case of comparison envy, and it wasn't pretty. It only left me feeling sorry for myself. Rather than showing concern for the less fortunate, I languished in a puddle of self-pity. I had no peripheral vision for the margins.

That changed when, at eighteen, during the summer after my high school graduation, I volunteered to go on a short-term mission trip to Toronto with my church youth group. Our youth leader, Jeff, signed up to take a team of twelve on a weeklong service project with the Center for Student Missions. The white church bus pulled out of the parking lot on the Fourth of July, 1999. I played cards and sang songs with the rest of the group during the six-hour drive across Michigan and into Ontario, Canada, oblivious to how much the coming week would impact my life.

As our bus crossed the threshold into the inner city, we saw striking differences in architecture and landscape compared to our hometown. Trash littered roadside gutters. Bright graffiti colored run-down walls. Homeless people languished on ratty blankets spread across stained concrete. I tried not to stare.

When we arrived at our host church, the person in charge corralled our group into a basement hall for orientation. A big black guy wearing a backward baseball cap introduced himself as Mike. "I'll be looking after you guys while you're here. First on our agenda is a prayer tour of the city. My coworker, Jill, will be our tour guide. We're gonna drive around, show you guys some sights, tell you about our ministry, and pray for some key areas in the city." We all nodded and clambered back into the hot bus. The open windows weren't enough to diffuse the strong smell of sweaty teenagers.

As we drove through the city, helplessness choked me in two ways: first, by realizing there was nothing I alone could do that would impact or change this huge city in the slightest bit; and second, by realizing that if anything happened to me (like getting mugged), I could do nothing about it. My surroundings intimidated me.

At our first stop, Jill pointed to a small building. "That's called Kasey House," she explained. "It houses fourteen AIDS patients. The average length of a patient's stay before death is thirty-four days. They are not accepting of Christians." We prayed.

Jill called the next stop "Romper Room"—a child prostitution corner. "This corner is frequented by girls between the ages of twelve and fifteen, but they're usually not regulars." My stomach churned. We cried out to God on their behalf.

We stopped and prayed at a men's shelter called Seaton House. "Residents call this place 'Satan House,'" Jill told us. "Most people would rather sleep on the streets." Our bus driver turned a corner. Two blocks later, we were on South Drive—a wealthy neighborhood where houses started at a million dollars. The contrast jarred me.

When we got back to the church, someone on our team forgot to lock the bus door. We realized it soon afterward, but by then, somebody had stolen a camera, church money, a wallet, a CD player, and other belongings. We definitely weren't in Holland anymore.

One hot afternoon, we took the subway to a bus station where Mike addressed our group: "Okay, if you were on the streets, where would you sleep? What would you do for entertainment? Where would you get money? How would you get food?" We all looked at each other blankly. Mom's modest house back in Holland suddenly seemed like a mansion. I vowed under my breath never to complain again about my circumstances.

On one street, Mike sent us down into an underground store that served fifteen- to twenty-three-year-olds. The glass-encased counters displayed cigarettes, knives, and other drug and weapon paraphernalia for sale. When we climbed the stairs to street level, Mike asked, "Did any of you notice the black curtain in the back of that shop?" We shook our heads. "Well, behind that curtain is a movie theatre. Young girls go there to get drugs to sell so they can have money. They go into the theatre with older men and get paid depending on their performance." I didn't know whether I wanted to cry or throw up. Life seemed so dark. So dirty. So desperate.

In the seven days I spent immersed in inner-city life, I learned more raw details about prostitution, sexuality, and homelessness than I ever wanted to know. My worldview expanded like the reach of the sun's rays sliding over the horizon at dawn. This exposure shed new light on my circumstances, and for the first time, I saw that brokenness was not limited to my little corner of the universe. I wasn't the only one with a fragmented family. Hurt and heartache were prevalent in the city of Toronto too—but far worse than any pain I'd endured. God used the experience to put me in my place. It was as if He were telling me, "Stop whining about your past. Look at what you have compared to other people in the world. Stop saying, 'It's not fair,' and start saying, 'Thank you.'"

Glimpsing such harsh circumstances in Toronto taught me that home is not a guarantee. Even the Son of God had no place to lay His head (Matt. 8:20, Luke 9:58). Home is a gift—a gift I'd taken for granted. Years later, a sermon further pierced my conscience. From the pulpit, the pastor challenged, "Don't pity the one who has no home. Pity the one whose home or other possession is preventing him from being with Christ."

Years after our week in Toronto, I asked my youth pastor what he remembered about our trip. Among other memories, he surprised me with this: "It was on that trip that I knew beyond a shadow of a doubt that God was calling you to spend some time on the mission field in the near future. I remember your heart both breaking for some of the people we met and lighting up when given the opportunity to share God's love with them, even if it was only through a smile or a peanut butter sandwich. Watching you so naturally slide into your element was definitely a highlight of my trip."

I smiled, as I definitely would not have called it "sliding into my element" at the time. I knew I'd been irrevocably changed. My heart stirred with a new passion to bring the hope of Jesus to those who didn't have it—but much of my time in Toronto was spent with fear as a close companion. I was out of my comfort zone and scared, yet something about the anxiety made me feel more alive. My nervousness made me notice more of my surroundings—and in the noticing, I saw evidence of God. My "safe" existence in the quiet, familiar suburb of

Holland, Michigan, rarely pushed me into dependence on the Lord. I could coast through my days quite smoothly on my own. But in the heart of Toronto, I held the Lord close—or maybe He held me.

I soon found myself buried under books in my first semester at Hope College, a Christian liberal arts school in my hometown. Though not a wise financial move, I chose to live in a dorm on campus—my first small but significant step of independence. I roomed with Erin, a strong Christian friend from high school with a contagious enthusiasm for the Lord. Early in the school year, Erin got me an office job at Lakeland Community Church, where her parents worked. I started attending services with them as well, to get to know the church body I was serving. Until then, I'd attended the same church my whole life. While I still adored my home church family, it was invigorating to be welcomed so wholeheartedly by a new branch of believers. A collective vibe of spiritual fervor and passion swept through the church community. I couldn't help but get caught up in the wave of earnest devotion to God.

Through Erin's influence, my involvement at Lakeland Church, exposure to regular Bible teaching in chapel services on campus, and frequent spiritual conversations with friends and acquaintances, my wobbly commitment to Christ solidified that year. I started to see the goodness and mercy of God with fresh eyes, realizing He was in control of *everything*. While I had previously relegated God's lordship to church-related events, I became aware of His rule over every day of the week. My separation of sacred and secular began to blur. I slowly discovered that every aspect of life could become an act of worship.

Then one evening, a non-Christian guy friend called. "My parents are out of town. Do you wanna come over?" Without a second thought, I slammed my textbook shut and grabbed my car keys. At his house, we turned off the lights and turned on a movie and made out until the final credits rolled. As I drove back to campus later that night, God opened my eyes to my hypocrisy. As much as I tried to ignore my nagging conscience, the Lord made His message clear: I had to pick a side. I couldn't just act like a believer when I felt like it. If I called myself a Christian, I had to be fully committed, or not at all. Back in my dorm room, I climbed up to my lofted bed and weighed my options. Lying on my twin mattress on an ordinary weeknight, God gave me the grace to choose life.

The next morning, I told Erin about the turning point in my spiritual life. Her genuine enthusiasm spurred me on and confirmed that I'd made the right choice. She shared the news with her dad, who was one of the pastors at Lakeland. Thrilled, he asked me, "Do you want to be baptized? You know, to commemorate your recommitment to the Lord." Having grown up in a church that baptized infants, the thought never would have crossed my mind—yet something prompted me to consider his words carefully. I thought and prayed about the possibility for several days.

From the first mention, my heart inclined toward yes, except for one roadblock—my dad's girlfriend, Angela. I still hadn't forgiven her for being the wedge that drove my parents apart. I knew God wanted me to let it go. But I'd harbored bitterness in my heart for so many years, I couldn't imagine living without its familiar presence. The Holy Spirit kept prompting me to hand over the burden and forgive, but I ignored His nudges and decided that yes, baptism was the perfect sign to mark this new beginning.

My mom was taken aback when I told her. She challenged my decision. "But you were already baptized as a baby! What's the point of doing it again?" I tried to explain, but stopped short of revealing the double life I'd been living. I simply told her that I wanted to publicly profess my devotion to Jesus and my personal commitment to follow Him. "But isn't that exactly what you did six years ago, when you were confirmed in seventh grade?" I nodded, but held my ground.

Despite her mixed feelings, Mom came to Lakeland Church the morning I was baptized. Even my dad came to watch. My nerves worked overtime. I stood in front of the congregation and read my testimony before stepping into the hot tub positioned on stage for the occasion. The moment felt surreal, as if time slowed down. The pastor placed his arm behind my shoulders and dunked me backward into the water. I came up with a surge of adrenaline, bursting with gratitude to God for the gift of life—not only His goodness in this life, but His promise of the life to come.

Hope College offered twenty different mission trip opportunities during spring break, only three of which were international. After my Toronto experience, I was eager to see more of the world. After waiting in line overnight for a space on the popular trips, I scored the second to last spot on the Honduras team.

The following weeks included regular meetings with our team of fifteen. On March 17, 2000, after months of training and fund-raising, our departure day finally arrived. We left Hope College at two a.m. in a bus bound for Chicago. At six a.m., we flew from Chicago to Houston, and then on to Tegucigalpa, Honduras.

The landing strip in Tegucigalpa was a mix of dirt and gravel. As the pilot activated the brakes, the plane jerked and skidded, struggling to decelerate. We bobbed up and down and held on tight as the aircraft met bump after bump. Finally, the plane skidded to a stop. As we walked through the aircraft door and down the steps, we gasped when we realized where the plane had stopped. Just in front of us we saw a strip of bright orange flags serving as a barrier. And just beyond the flags was a steep cliff.

After we deplaned, I noticed a multitude of Hondurans standing in the rundown airport, staring at our stark-white faces. It was my first time in a foreign country full of nonwhites. I wanted to shrink into my skin or at least cover myself with something. Anything to make me feel less conspicuous.

Traffic laws were virtually nonexistent. Honking was the only noticeable common road practice, used liberally to warn someone that you were about to hit them. The roads weren't paved, only dirt—which also meant no lane markings. At any given time, three cars could be racing to "claim" the lane that wouldn't have to stop and wait for oncoming cars to pass. None of the drivers slowed down out of courtesy—they all just sped up and forced other cars to slam on their brakes at the last minute.

Fruit stands and carts selling handmade crafts lined the dirt roads. Women walked the streets with huge baskets balanced atop their heads. In lieu of standalone billboards, long rock faces along the street shoulders displayed painted advertisements.

The biggest culture shock hit when I saw the so-called "houses." My mouth hung open at the scrap pieces roughly assembled to resemble shacks. Many didn't even have roofs; those that did were only partially covered. Instead of glass covering the windows, metal bars let the fresh air in and kept thieves out. Besides the condition of the shacks, the roughly hewn structures were stacked on top of each other all the way up the hillsides, like awkward teenagers trying to form a pyramid by kneeling on each other's backs. A single, long staircase served as the only way to access the residences.

We stayed with a missionary couple from Michigan who had been serving in Honduras for over a decade. Across the street lived a family with four small children. Every time we walked past them, they scrambled into a line against a wall and yelled, *"Un foto! Un foto!"* begging us to take their picture. The abandoned shell of a rusty red hatchback parked next to their house served as the children's only source of entertainment.

During our week in Honduras, we spent much of our time finishing classrooms for a new school. We primed and painted inside and out, and made blackboards and corkboards. We visited a clinic and a cashew farm, learning more about the culture and economy each day. We got to meet a number of locals at a church service, on bus rides, and in the marketplaces. My four years of Spanish paid off, and it was a joy to converse with the people I met. Despite their circumstances—whether they labored for hours in the heat, pounding out cashew nuts from their fruit encasings, or scrubbing soiled linens in an overcrowded, smelly clinic—the people seemed content. Most had so little, yet radiated kindness. Their bright, colorful clothing mirrored the joy in their faces.

The inauguration of my passport did more than serve as a rite of passage. Honduras shaped the next piece in my worldview puzzle, formulating a larger picture than I knew as a child. Differences in culture and lifestyle challenged my narrow-mindedness as I experienced the richness of diversity. Until I traveled out of my white, suburban bubble, I naively believed my way of doing things must be the way everyone did things. As I sat for nearly three hours in a church service without hearing a word of English, my former "one way only" mind-set was slashed to pieces. Yes, Jesus remained the only way to salvation (John 14:6), but I had limited the way He could be worshipped. The Honduran men and women glorifying God all around me—these were my brothers and sisters.

I started to feel as though my upbringing had cheated me. I adored the faces that filled my home church pews week after week—but they were so monochromatic. I felt as if the body I'd known my whole life had been missing limbs all along. I now saw that the perimeter of home as I knew it was far too exclusive. Too much the same. It was time to break down some walls to let more of God's people in. Even if some of the breaking involved my own heart.

CHAPTER 6

FORGIVEN

"Nothing in my hand I bring, simply to Thy cross I cling."

—Augustus M. Toplady, "Rock of Ages"

I'd love to say that I had some deep, spiritual encounter that confirmed my calling to become a missionary, but it was actually quite the opposite. My second semester at Hope College was underway, and although my spiritual life had grown muscle, I still didn't know where God was leading me. I hadn't declared a major, and my class load wasn't providing any clarity.

One day as I drove alone in my metallic sky-blue '99 Ford Escort, the song "Africa" by the band Toto came on the radio. I barely knew the lyrics, but belted out my own version nonetheless, making sure I hit the chorus right. And suddenly, it clicked. *That's it.* It was Africa that I wanted. Looking back, it was a bizarre moment. I had no idea what I was walking into—but God did. Of course, the song couldn't possibly reflect the Africa I would come to know and love, yet that was what God used to spark my desire and open my heart to the possibility.

In subsequent years, I watched the hearts of friends and missionaries burn for certain areas. It seemed that the Lord placed different yearnings in different lives. Some of my friends acted on their desire to serve in the Philippines; others prepared to live in Central Asia. Some poured their lives into North Africa, while others raised orphan awareness in Ukraine. For me, the pull of Africa refused to let up. The feeling of being "called" was difficult to articulate. It wasn't synonymous with desire, but rather a surety that this was the right path, and I must pursue it—whether it made sense or not; whether I wanted to or not.

Doing my best to obey, I scoured the internet researching various mission agencies in Africa. I felt my attention drawn to the nation of Kenya, so I filled out forms and applied for a two-year internship opportunity. My stomach turned a little as I mailed the envelope, wondering if I could really live in a hut with no running water. Some days I tried to persuade myself that staying perched on my comfortable cushion called West Michigan was the best option. But deep down, I knew it wasn't true for me.

It took a secular song to make me aware, but the conviction had been present for a while. A latent seed buried deep in the soil, waiting to be watered. In the span of a song, it broke through the surface and reached for the sun. Like the unhurried growth of a new plant, God slowly but progressively revealed the path set before me. Following meant a series of small steps. Saying yes to Him during my confirmation in front of my church. Yes to Toronto. Yes to Hope College. He didn't ask me to lunge headfirst into the unknown. He waited to reveal the next brick in the pavement, and then stepped out in front of me to show that it was a safe place to land. His presence already waited ahead.

But then He laid a fork in the road. One trail had a sign that read "missions" in bold letters. The other was unmarked. As much as I strained my neck and squinted my eyes, I couldn't see farther than a few feet down either path. Apprehension built as I lifted my foot. Then God turned my face toward the marked path and nudged me forward. And the trajectory of my life was forever altered.

After feeling called to Africa, I floundered around trying to figure out the next step. I never heard back about the two-year Kenya internship application and wasn't quite sure how to handle the silence. I still felt persuaded that God was leading me to Africa, but all I could see was a closed door. I wrestled in prayer with God and aloud with my roommate, Erin. One afternoon I got back to our dorm after a full day of classes and found this note on my desk:

Dearest Kate, I know this has been a crazy semester for you. It seems like this whole calling thing has been tugging on your heart a lot. I just want you to know that I'm praying for you, that God speaks clearly to you. When He does that, you can be confident with any decision you

*make. As always, I'm behind you 100% no matter what
you decide. Let me know if you need to talk or pray about
anything. Don't be discouraged with people who misun-
derstand you. Have faith. I know that you will be awe-
some like none other with whatever you do! I love you.*

—Erin

Proverbs 3:5–6

Her support meant the world to me. Weeks passed
as I tried to discern the way forward. Eventually, God
turned my attention to Kuyper College in Grand Rapids,
Michigan, about forty-five minutes away. The school
offered a major in cross-cultural missions, and their tuition was a fraction of what I was paying at Hope.

It was one of the most gut-wrenching decisions
of my young adult life. I loved Hope College. I loved
my roommate, the people I'd met, my dorm, the social
life . . . everything. Not only did I get to live with my
best friend, I still dwelled in the familiar arms of my
beloved hometown. But if I was going to pursue missions, Hope College was not the best option in terms
of course offerings or tuition. Racking up tens of thousands of dollars in debt was not an ideal way to enter
the mission field.

I didn't want to leave Hope, yet the tug I felt in the
reservoir of my soul was too strong to resist. I concluded
it had to be from God. I surrendered my comfort and
desires to His nudging and declared myself, after many
tears, a cross-cultural missions major at Kuyper College
the following year. I knew no one at the new school. It felt
like a step backward. My stomach knotted at the thought

of meeting new people all over again and adjusting to new campus rules and professors' expectations.

My dad, who had previously teased me about wanting to be a "starving artist," balked at the prudence of becoming a missionary. "Dad," I retorted, only somewhat in jest. "I will never in my lifetime know everything there is to know about the Bible, and until Jesus returns, there will always be more people who need to know about Him, so—perfect job security."

Despite my initial temper tantrum toward God about having to switch schools, He pleasantly surprised me at Kuyper. The professors, staff, and my fellow students were incredibly kind. The school consisted of about three hundred students—ten percent of the student body at Hope. The small size meant it was easy to get to know most people, and I soon found a new home away from home.

I soaked up Bible college like a sponge and was shaped more spiritually and theologically in those two years than my previous nineteen years combined. At first I battled jealousy toward all the kids who came to Kuyper with Christian school backgrounds. They already knew all the books of the Bible in order and had even learned how to share the gospel in Spanish as part of their foreign language curriculum. I felt embarrassed by how behind I was. Slowly but surely, my brain made friends with big words like *justification* and *sanctification*, *Calvinism* and *Arminianism*, *eschatology* and *dispensationalism*.

Rich discussions with classmates trumped the cheap midnight coffee at Steak 'n Shake, and spilled into games of Ping-Pong and euchre. Debates bounced back and forth for days over topics like election and predes-tination, baptism, and the role of women in the church. Professors and newfound friends challenged me to work out my salvation with fear and trembling (Phil. 2:12) to "be prepared in season and out of season" (2 Tim. 4:2) and to "always be prepared to give an answer to everyone who asks you to give the reason for the hope that you have" (1 Pet. 3:15). I learned about apologetics, and how to defend my developing faith from the flaming arrows con-tinually fired by the devil.

My sister, Sarah, came for Siblings Weekend in October, and I proudly introduced her to my new friends as I showed her around campus. Now that we weren't sharing a room (or even a house) anymore, our teenage spats had subsid-ed and each passing month seemed to draw us closer as friends. She would be heading off to college herself the following year, and I was missing out on important events of her high school career. I hadn't seen a single one of her tennis matches that fall. Our brief weekend together in a setting without Mom made me realize that we were both becoming adults, forming a unique bond that transcend-ed our "growing up" years. Little did I know how heavily I would depend on that bond in decades to come.

At Kuyper, the entire campus gathered to worship at chapel services every Monday, Wednesday, and Friday morning. Various professors and guest speakers took turns sharing a message after the student-led singing.

During one chapel service, my missions professor stood up to speak. Instead of a usual sermon, he stepped off the stage and leaned in close to the front row of students, scanning each face intently. His prolonged silence set the congregation on edge.

"Today we're going to spend some time in quiet reflection," he announced after a long pause. "Get yourselves into a posture of humility. Maybe that means getting down on your knees or bowing your head. Maybe it means moving out of the pew and finding a different place to sit. Ask God to prepare your heart to listen."

I could feel my heart thudding a little harder against the walls of my chest. I squirmed in my seat. What was this all about? A few people shifted to new positions; some knelt on the carpeted floor, hands folded for prayer.

My professor went on. "For the next twenty minutes, we're going to be completely silent. No talking, no whispering. Just be still. Give God the space to fill the void. Ask Him to open your ears to hear Him. Pay attention to where He leads your thoughts."

Twenty minutes? Was he serious? I balked at the outlandish idea.

"I'm going to stop talking in just a moment," my professor continued. "But before I do, I want you to pay special attention to an area in your life that is hindering you from growing closer to God. Ask the Lord to reveal anything that is blocking you from growing in your relationship with Him."

Angela. My mind and heart knew it right away. But, as in years past, I shoved the thought out of my head. *Yeah, I know, God,* I said cheekily. *But besides that, what else?*

Angela. The answer was clear. It wasn't going away.

Lord, I know you want me to forgive Angela, but I can't. I know I can't. It's impossible. My anger and bitterness have been there for too long. They've become part of the fiber of my being. So let's just move on to the second thing in line behind her. What else is blocking me from growing closer to you besides my inability to forgive her?

Angela. I sighed in frustration. This wasn't going well. I looked at my watch. Not even five minutes had passed. I felt trapped. Cornered. Did my professor plan this just to spite me?

The clock slowed down. Seconds ticked by with agonizing lethargy. I tried to think about other things. Anything. My New Testament assignment due later in the week. What I planned to eat for dinner that night. How many pews lined the sanctuary. Anything. But the thought kept crawling back to the forefront of my mind: *You have to forgive her. It's time. You can't put it off any longer. It's been too long already. You're not going to grow any closer to God if you don't remove this roadblock.*

I inhaled a deep breath of resignation and exhaled a long sigh of surrender.

Fine, I prayed. *You win. I'll do it. But I don't want to. But wait—how does this work? Can I just tell you I forgive her in my heart and be done with it? I mean, nobody else has to know—it's just between you and me. Okay. Good. I forgive her. There. I said it. You happy now?*

Call her.

My stomach knotted. *No. No way. I'm sorry, but that's just asking too much. No. N. O.*

Call her.

Oh my GOSH, can I PLEASE get out of here now? Isn't the twenty minutes up? This is ridiculous!

That's the only way to be free of this burden.

My head hung low, chin to my chest. I kept my eyes closed, afraid that if anyone saw them open, they would see right through me.

Another long exhale, and with it went my resolve.

I wiped a stray tear, took another long breath through my nose, and prayed, *Fine.*

Chapel ended, and I shuffled in a stupor all the way to my Doctrine class. I couldn't think straight for the rest of the day. I couldn't even eat at lunch. I was too nervous. Terrified, actually. *What would she say? Would she get mad? Hang up on me? Yell? Chew me out and tell me what a wretch I'd been for the past twelve years?*

Maybe I could still back out. Tell God we could try again some other time. But God had been chipping at my hardened heart for over a decade, and that day, He finally split it wide open. After my last class of the day, I slowly made my way back to my dorm. My legs felt heavier. Every part of my body knew the task that lay before me, and each appendage protested. The dorms bustled with noise and activity, so I picked up my black cordless phone and trudged outside. From the sidewalk in front of the brick residential building, my finger reluctantly dialed Dad and Angela's landline number.

My heart pounded loud into the receiver. *Ring . . . ring.*

I considered hanging up.

"Hello?" It was Angela.

"Hi Angela, it's Kate."

"Oh, your dad's not here. Do you want me to have him call you back when he gets home?"

My breath caught in my throat. I swallowed hard and took a step backward, shocked that she just assumed I was calling for my dad without me even asking for him. But of course. When did I ever call to talk to her?

"Um, actually . . ." I didn't even recognize my own voice. It shook as much as the receiver in my hand. "Actually, I wasn't calling for him. I was calling to talk to you."

"Oh!" Clearly, it was her turn to be surprised.

"Umm…" I didn't know how or where to start. "Well, I was just calling to say sorry."

Silence. Then, "For what?" Genuine confusion transmitted across the line.

"For everything. I've been really mean to you ever since we met. I treated you badly, and I'm sorry." I started to cry. "I guess I was just mad because I blamed you for my parents' divorce. But still, it wasn't fair. I shouldn't have been so rude." Snot dripped out of my nose while I searched my pockets for a Kleenex. Nothing. I didn't even check to see if anyone was looking, I just wiped it with the back of my sleeve. Fear loomed large as I waited for a response, sniffling loudly and patting tears with my wrist.

Then I heard the unexpected: more sniffles, but not my own. Was Angela crying too?

I pushed out the hardest words of all: "Will you please forgive me?"

"Oh, yes. Of course I forgive you," she gushed through her own tears. "I love you. You know that, right?"

The words sounded foreign but safe. My response snuck up on me: "I love you too." And then further shock: I meant it.

We both laughed the awkward, airy laugh that shows up when words run out.

"Thank you," I added sincerely.

"Thank *you*," Angela replied, still sniffling.

And then we hung up.

Immediately, the oddest sensation swept over me. I felt so light. Like an actual, physical weight had been lifted right off my shoulders. My burden was gone. I laughed out loud. I looked around, suddenly aware that I wasn't the only person on campus. I'd been so consumed in the bubble of my phone conversation, I hadn't noticed anyone else passing by. But now I needed to tell someone what had just happened to me. I was bursting with firsthand experience that had to be shared—forgiveness was for real. It wasn't just a figment of my imagination. It was an actual, real thing that God used to set people free. And He did it for me.

CHAPTER 7

INDIA

"Give thanks to the LORD, call on his name;
make known among the nations what he has done."

—Psalm 105:1

In October 2000, just two months into my first year at Kuyper, I went on a mission trip to India. The Lakeland Church staff knew of my newly developed plan to pursue missions, so they invited me to join a team of twelve for a two-week trip. We planned to do evangelism, gospel teaching, and worship ministry at a believers' conference organized by the Gospel Association of India in Vijayawada, a city in the southeastern state of Andhra Pradesh.

I'd never seen such poverty in my life. The stench of it clung to the back of my throat, the density of odors changing with every turn. Sleeping bodies dotted the concrete train platform when we arrived. We stepped gingerly, careful not to trip over anyone. I cringed and felt guilty both for having a home and for wishing I were there. Suddenly several young Indian men wearing red uniforms appeared. Our team leader Marty explained, "They're called *cooleys*. They're here to help us. Now watch this." The men worked quickly. One wrapped a white towel on top of his head, kind of like a flat turban, while another heaved a suitcase up onto the first man's head. Then another suitcase. And *another*. Three enormous suitcases stacked on top of each other, and the guy walked off like it was nothing.

Like Honduras, the traffic in India was insane. No traffic rules, just a game of chicken between two speeding, doorless rickshaws to see who would swerve first. My life flashed before my eyes regularly. Focusing on the bobbing plastic statues of Hindu gods affixed to the taxi dashboards didn't exactly give me comfort, either. Three of us sat on the single bench seat across the back while our driver controlled the accelerator and brakes from the handle bars. I gaped through the open rickshaw at women sitting sidesaddle on motorcycles, hands folded in their laps. Whenever our taxi stopped, Indian people crowded around, begging for food and money. I wanted to give them something—a home, a better life. Prayer became my only language.

As we drove, we crossed a bridge over the Krishna River. Peering down, we saw hordes of people standing knee-deep in the river—some bathing, some peeing, some beating dirty clothes against large, protruding rocks. Colorful garments covered the banks, drying in the sun before the owners shook the dust off. I would never take my shower, washing machine, or tumble dryer for granted again.

The next day, we visited a prestigious all-girls college about an hour away. I found it easier than expected to share my testimony through a Telugu translator. After speaking, several girls crowded around me. One pleaded with wide black eyes: "Tell me more about Jesus." Other girls dressed in bright fuchsia, orange, and turquoise saris mirrored her earnest desire. Their eagerness to know more about God and His Word made me wish Americans shared the same enthusiasm.

India was my first experience pouring bottled water over my toothbrush, trying to remember not to swallow anything that came out of a faucet. My first time not having a toilet to sit on. Squatting over an open hole in the floor of a train carriage, watching the tracks rush past between my unsteady feet.

It was also the first time I could recall being treated as outrageously superior because of my skin's paleness. I had been keenly aware of my whiteness in Honduras, but the beautiful, smiling Indian people crowded around us in awe, touching our hair, stroking our clothes. Pleading with their eyes and hands for us to pray over them. Despite the language barrier, their message was clear: they thought we were closer to God. They thought our prayers were more powerful than their own. Every day felt like a reenactment of the story in the Gospels when the bleeding woman reached out to touch Jesus's cloak (Mark 5:25–34).

And it felt so wrong.

I was no better than the desperate souls crowding into the building to hear the worship music and gospel teaching night after night—yet I didn't know how to communicate the truth in a way they would understand.

During our regular worship sessions, the men and women sat barefoot on separate sides of the hall, having removed their shoes at the door because they were about to step on holy ground. As soon as the pastor approached the microphone and said, "Let's pray," every person in the hall fell to his or her knees with faces to the ground. My lack of physical display of reverence toward the Lord shamed me. While the pastor prayed aloud through the sound system's speakers, each bowed head prayed his or her own prayers aloud as well. In glorious harmony, the prayers of the saints rose to the heavens. A sweet aroma to the One enthroned above. *This is what God gets to hear all the time,* I marveled. Peering out from my place on the stage, I saw beauty radiated from every soul. And I saw the Church. All different colors, cultures, and backgrounds worshipping one God as one body with one voice. A rush of giddiness coursed through me as I caught a tiny glimpse of heaven.

After each session, our team had the opportunity to pray one-on-one with any who approached us. Women flocked to the ladies in our group, asking for healing, lifting their saris to expose ailing body parts. Through translators, they requested prayer for everything from headaches to heart problems, infertility to indigestion. I felt awkward and out of place. I wanted to slip out of the crowd, back to the hotel, back to the comfort of my own house and culture.

One afternoon, we witnessed fifty men and women being baptized in a small pool outside the meeting place. Fear plastered the women's faces as they were immersed into the shallow water. I expected them to be filled with joy. "Why do they look so afraid?" I whispered to Marty. "Don't they understand what baptism means?"

"They *do* understand. That's why they're so afraid. By taking this step of faith, these women will go home changed. From this day on, their husbands will beat them every time they leave the house, because the men don't approve of their wives going to church."

In stark contrast to the Spirit-filled worship and wholehearted commitments to Christ we witnessed, much of the trip was thick with spiritual oppression. It pressed heavy on my chest. We saw women and children with shaved heads, having walked long distances to sacrifice their hair to Hindu gods—the highest offering a female could give. Temples and shrines crowded my vision at every turn. I craved escape.

After twelve long days overseas, I arrived home full and empty. Resolved to pursue cross-cultural missions and questioning whether I could cope. I felt physically, emotionally, and spiritually drained—but after what I had seen, how could I spend the rest of my life coasting through middle-class American ease? The fervent devotion I'd witnessed in the Indian Christians and the beauty of multiple cultures in worship spurred my heart to a new depth of understanding and gospel urgency. And yet, upon entering my house, I wanted to fall down and kiss the carpet. It felt so good to be home. I missed my mom. I missed silverware. And toilets. And tap water.

I felt safe again. Comfortable. Protected. Could I really pursue a career that would make me leave all this behind?

Exhausted, I opened my suitcase and fell backward at the stench that emerged. "Ugh, gross!" I groaned as my mom looked on. It was late, and we were both tired.

"Why don't you just carry the dirty clothes downstairs to the laundry room, and we can take care of it tomorrow?" Mom suggested.

I was nervous that foreign germs clung to my garments and didn't want to risk infecting the rest of the house. Instead of dumping the whole suitcase downstairs, I bundled up the clothes into a black garbage bag, tied it closed, and set it in our garage, just next to the door. My plan was to get a good night's sleep, then disinfect the reeking clothes first thing in the morning.

I slept like a rock. Waking in a haze, I couldn't believe it was almost noon. The travel and time change had wrecked me. I decided to shower before tackling the laundry. Reaching into my drawer, I couldn't find any clean underwear. *Great*, I thought. *I must have packed all of it for my two weeks in India. I guess I won't be taking a shower first.*

I opened the door to the garage to haul the garbage bag of clothes downstairs to the washing machine. It wasn't there. *Oh, that was nice of her. I bet Mom started my laundry already.* I walked down the stairs to the laundry room. No black bag. No clothes. Now I was confused. I walked back up in search of my mom.

"Mom, did you see a black garbage bag in the garage?"

"Oh, yeah!" she replied cheerfully. "I took it out to the street this morning for the garbage man to pick up. It's trash day today."

I burst out laughing. "All my clothes were in there! *Everything!*"

Mom gasped. "Oh, honey, I am *so* sorry—I had no idea!" She rushed to the window to see if the garbage truck had come already. It had. Two weeks' worth of clothes, gone. All we could do was laugh—until we went to the store and saw how much it cost to replace two weeks of undergarments. Yet because of all that I'd witnessed in India, my grip on my possessions had loosened. Clothes didn't seem to matter as much as they did before I left. Besides, I was home—and that was all that mattered.

India made me a more grateful person. Grateful for clean water. Grateful for my own bed. For a toilet that flushed. And most of all, grateful for the gift of faith in Christ. I thanked God for the chance to see His church from a whole new perspective. Indian Christians put my own feeble faith to shame—they prayed with such expectancy, believing wholeheartedly that God would hear and answer. Their dedication to the Lord and willingness to stand for Him in spite of guaranteed opposition challenged me to plant my flag more visibly for the one who hung on a cross and died for me.

But outside the church walls, apart from the passionate believers, I saw far too many dead souls walking dirty streets—empty and lost. I desperately wanted God to make them alive as He had done for me. I wanted them to know they could be saved by grace, not by shaving their heads and sacrificing their hair. I saw the intricate architecture of their temples and shrines and wanted them to see that the "God who made the world and everything in it is the Lord of heaven and earth and does not live in temples built by human hands." To know that in Christ and through faith in Christ they could "approach God with freedom and confidence." To see and believe that with Jesus's blood, He "purchased men for God from every tribe and language and people and nation." I wanted them to look at their poverty and know the glorious riches that could be theirs in Christ Jesus, who meets all their needs. To look at their country and long for a better one—a heavenly one. I ached for the day when every knee will bow and every tongue confess that Jesus Christ is Lord.[1]

CHAPTER 8

DIRECTION

*"In his heart a man plans his course,
but the LORD determines his steps."*

—Proverbs 16:9

During my first year at Kuyper, I landed a part-time job at a nearby city mission called Mel Trotter, a residential shelter that housed men on one side of the building, and women and children on the other. My role was to help with the children and youth, particularly with the after-school program. Those kids melted me.

I was there five days a week after school, helping in the computer lab, assisting with homework, playing group games, chatting about life. Every Monday the staff received a printed sheet with a list of current residents. The number of children fluctuated from twenty to seventy. Each week my eyes scanned the page, and inevitably, my heart sank. More families moved out over the weekend, unexpectedly. Without a good-bye. Children who had hung their stories and smiles on my heart, gone. New names filled their place. Names without faces yet. Names with brokenness trailing behind. Names I would grow to love.

As I spent week after week ministering to homeless kids, something poked and prodded at my insides. It just wouldn't leave me alone. I could feel the divide between residents and staff. "Them" and "us." I didn't think that was how Jesus did it—just clocked in at eight or nine in the morning and then punched his time card at five to go home. After thinking and praying about it for a while, I made a decision.

It certainly wasn't anything I would've come up with on my own. The Lord gave me the desire, in my own context and as best as I could, to emulate the incarnational ministry of Christ. To become one of the homeless. To dwell with them, among them. To meet them at their point of need—not just show up for eight hours, pretend I understood, and go back to a life of middle-class luxury and comfort.

In a highly uncharacteristic move, I asked my supervisor if I could live at the mission for the summer. She just looked at me, slack-jawed, in her office, as if she wasn't sure she'd heard me correctly. "I'm sorry, you want to do *what*?" With a wavering voice, I repeated my desire to live in the women's wing of the homeless shelter. My boss sort of scoffed in surprise and said she would have to talk to the rest of the leadership team and get back to me.

The leadership agreed, stunned as they all were, so on May 14, 2001, I packed up my necessities and moved into a single room for the summer. When my supervisor opened the door to the room that would be mine for the next fourteen weeks, I hesitated before stepping in. Was this really a good idea? As I crossed the threshold, the starkness startled me. A twin bed, a wooden dresser, and my suitcase were the only items in the room. No bedside table. No lamp. No desk. No mirror. Just the bed and some drawers. *At least I have my own room*, I thought. Then suddenly a loneliness swept over me. Isolation. I was alone there. Third-shift staff worked nights, but no other employees slept in the building. Only the residents who had nowhere else to go.

The first few nights I dozed off and on, tossing back and forth in fitful spurts. Loud voices in the hallways paid no respect to sleep. Yelling matches between residents startled me awake every couple of hours, my heart beating out of my chest as I lurched out of shallow slumber, wondering where I was and why I was there.

In my first week, my boss sat me down in her office. "You realize you can't get emotionally involved with the residents' issues, right? Don't take anything personally. You have to maintain a distance from them. You need to make sure they see the clear line that separates you as a staff member, not their friend."

I resisted and resented her instructions. The "rules" defeated the purpose of my presence. I wanted to erase the line, or at least blur it. But blurring would come back to bite me. I quickly learned just how easily and often the residents took advantage of me. At age nineteen, I'd never been in such a position of leadership and authority. Women twice my age had to listen to what I told them to do or not do. I was naïve and gullible, always giving the residents the benefit of the doubt. They saw my soft-ness and took me for a ride whenever they could. I had to remember that I was living in a rehabilitation facility. Many women sleeping in the rooms surrounding mine were there because every other homeless shelter in the city had already kicked them out. Mel Trotter was their last resort.

I tried to put myself in the residents' shoes, to see life from their perspective. Many of those dear ladies were desperate. Dependent. Needy. Exactly where God wanted them—and me—to be. Sometimes people need to hit rock bottom before they start looking up. Before they start looking beyond themselves, to the only true source of hope.

By moving into the shelter, I'd jumped into the deep end. It was sink or swim. I busted women for having drugs in their purse. I escorted Children's Protective Services to an interview with an unfit mother. I broke up fistfights and hair pulling spats, and visited one teenager's school, pleading with staff to let him pass seventh grade. They weren't swayed. A few kids swore at me and told me they didn't have to listen to me because I was white. I felt the sting of betrayal when one female resident I trusted was found writing out fake prescriptions from a stolen prescription pad.

But the joys countered the discouragements as I spent time with the kids all day, every day. In the middle of the playground one hot July afternoon, six-year-old Tynesha pulled on my shirt sleeve. "Miss Kate, I gots ta *use* it!"

"Use what, honey?" I glanced around us, wondering if she wanted to use the slide or the swings.

"I gots ta *use* it!"

"Use what?" The other kids started laughing.

"Miss Kate," Tynesha's older sister, Shaniqua, chimed in. "She gots ta use the *bathroom*!"

I ate my meals with the residents in the dining hall, discussing gospel issues over trays of cafeteria food. Most women were receptive but felt trapped by their circumstances. They had a hunch that God might be good, but didn't believe He would forgive them for what they'd done. Besides, if He loved them, why did He allow them to end up in this place? Some professed Christ and gave Him praise in the midst of their hardships. They radiated gratitude and bolstered my faith.

On the weekends, I cheated and went back to my mom's house. Every Friday night when I stepped through the front doors of the mission toward my waiting car, I felt guilty about my freedom to walk away from the system so easily and sorry for those who couldn't. Right next to the guilt lived a deep sense of relief as I inhaled the fresh air and shook off the pressures of the week.

That summer, I learned the value of home. Not to take it for granted. Home should be held loosely—not as a right, but as a gift. A precious gift from the hand of God, who gives a sweet bite of home now as a foretaste of what is to come.

God used my fourteen weeks living at Mel Trotter to remind me that people are different, but really we're all the same. We're all needy—in desperate need of grace and redemption, groaning to be clothed in our heavenly dwelling (2 Cor. 5:1-2). We're all living in a temporary homeless shelter, ready and waiting for something better—for a home that lasts.

September 2001 kicked off my third year of college. After meeting with an academic advisor early in the semester, I realized that after that school year, I would only have three classes left to obtain my degree. As it turned out, all three were only offered in the second semester of the following year, which meant I would have September through December 2002 with no course load.

After pondering the possibilities for those empty months I approached my missions professor and announced, "I want to go to Africa." I didn't care where. He nodded, scratched his beard, and suggested, "How about South Africa?"

I knew virtually nothing about the country of South Africa except that two of my fellow students were from there. Twin brothers Nathan and Jonathan were studying in the States for a year before heading back to their home country. Their dad was the director of a campus ministry called the Student YMCA in Cape Town, and one of their three campuses had no female staff worker. Would I like to volunteer for six months? I took a whole two seconds to think about it and said yes.

Once I decided to go, I made fast friends with Nathan and Jonathan. I was eager to learn as much as I could before they moved back to Cape Town three months later, when the semester ended in December. We sat in their room on campus as they proudly paged through a thick brochure from their high school alma mater, a prestigious all-boys school in the southern suburbs of Cape

Town. They pointed to posters taped to their dorm walls of the University of Cape Town, with its red rooftops nestled into the elbow of Devil's Peak, canopied by a perfectly blue sky. They even tried to teach me the proper surfing technique on their dorm room floor. We all practiced lying flat on our bellies and maneuvering to a standing position. Granted, it's a tad easier to get from stomach to feet on carpet than on a moving, floating board in a body of water. But still. They were determined, and I was a willing student.

Nathan and Jonathan showed me pictures of Table Mountain, named for its flat top, around which the rest of the city was built. "Sometimes a blanket of smooth, white clouds filters over the peak before fading away. We call those clouds the tablecloth," Nathan explained. "Devil's Peak is the pointier mountain just to the left when you're looking at Table Mountain, and Lion's Head is the smaller mound to the right. Can you see the shape of the lion's head right there?" he asked, pointing. "Behind Table Mountain are the Twelve Apostles—twelve separate peaks that jut out along the coast by Camps Bay beach. You can see them stretched out when you climb about two hours to the top of Table Mountain. Or you could take the cable car, but hiking is way more fun."

"Guess how many official languages we have," Jonathan prompted.

"Umm . . . four? Five? I have no idea."

"Eleven," he boasted. "Here, lemme teach you some." He proceeded to rattle off greetings in Afrikaans, isiXhosa and Sesotho. He imitated the English accents of the colored South Africans—a whole separate culture that formed predominantly from whites and blacks having children together illegally during apartheid.[1]

I soon learned that the twins' dad served on the board of a Bible college in Cape Town. After several email exchanges, I arranged to take my remaining three classes at the Bible Institute of South Africa. Through Nathan and Jonathan's parents, Gary and Liz, I also made contact with a man named Stefan, my future boss at the Student YMCA, and Alan, the pastor of the church I would attend with them. The warmth in Stefan and Alan's emails was nearly tangible through my computer screen.

With every story, my desire to leave for Africa grew stronger. The pride and passion Nathan and Jonathan possessed for their country was contagious. When they returned to Cape Town in December 2001, I spent the next six months poring over South African tour books, studying maps, highlighting points of interest to add to my bucket list. The photographs didn't portray the Africa I imagined. Rather than elephants lumbering in dusty red soil, I saw ostriches and baboons ambling along paved roads. Instead of outhouses and barefoot children, I saw infrastructure and a BMW pavilion. God used these images to challenge my stereotypes and increase my longing to go.

My plan was to stay in South Africa for five months, just long enough to complete my final three classes. I got a six-month study permit, and Kuyper even let me walk early at their May 2002 graduation ceremony. Back at my mom's house after graduation, I began to pack my life into two suitcases, agonizing over which items would make the cut. I laid out the candidates on my bedroom floor, teetering back and forth in indecision. *Should I take that framed picture? What about that sweater? Will I want that necklace while I'm there? What if it gets lost or stolen?* Airline regulations allowed me to check two suitcases weighing up to fifty pounds each. That's a hundred pounds of stuff I was convinced I couldn't live without. Stuff I hoped would remind me of home.

On July 1, 2002, I looked around my room and thought about not seeing my house for five whole months. Not sleeping in my bed. As I filtered through mementos and photos, clothes and shoes, reality sunk in.

In a matter of hours, I was moving to Africa.

CHAPTER 9

CAPE TOWN

*"The LORD will go before you,
the God of Israel will be your rear guard."*

—Isaiah 52:12

Nearly thirty-six hours after hugging my Mom and Sarah good-bye in the airport, after the first boarding call and four flights spanning three continents, I finally saw it for the first time.

South Africa.

Adrenaline pumped something fierce in the face of fatigue. I leaned in close to the cold airplane window, eager to catch a glimpse of my new home.

The pilot announced that we had some time to kill before being cleared for landing, so he decided to give us an aerial tour of the Cape Peninsula. I'd never seen anything like it. Rolling coastlines in greens and blues, sandy beaches dotted with boulders jutting into the surf. Atlantic whitecaps curled up into a grin: *"You're gonna like it here."* Rocky hills and mountains, forests interspersed with winding roads and strategically placed houses. It was as if the Lord was smiling down on me, or maybe winking from the sparkles in the sea. Whispering over the hum of the jetliner's engine, *"Look where I've brought you. Look what I've made for you to enjoy. Just look."* I was slack-jawed by the sheer glory of it all.

As the plane landed, Jonathan and his mom, Liz, greeted me in arrivals with a gift bag decorated with safari animals and the words "Welcome to South Africa" typed numerous times on every side. South African goodies filled the bag—a map of Cape Town, gummy candies called wine gums, dried jerky-like meat called biltong, a bag of licorice All-Sorts, and even a stand-up beaded doll with black, yarn-woven dreadlocks. In that single gesture, they blew me away with the warmth of their welcome.

My mind performed its first acrobatic shift when Liz got into the car on the right-hand side to drive and proceeded to steer the car into the left lane the whole way. On the ride from the airport to their home, Liz and Jonathan gave me a running commentary as fast as the car moved. My brain was on sensory and information overload, but a permanent smile plastered my face. I squinted from the bright sun and endless blue sky while trying to decipher the billboards advertising unknown brands like MTN and Vodacom. As the car followed a natural bend in the road, Table Mountain suddenly came into view. She looked like an old friend, though I'd only seen her from the airplane window less than an hour earlier.

As we drove along the N2 highway toward the southern suburbs, Liz and Jonathan pointed out the shacks and shanties that lined the busy route. I gawked out the passenger window at the masses of corrugated metal structures topped with cardboard, garbage bags, and rocks to hold down the makeshift roofs—lingering effects after decades of apartheid.

Within two hours of getting to their house, the phone rang. Liz answered before announcing it was for me. Surprised and somewhat confused, I took the receiver. "Hi Kate! It's Alan, pastor of Holy Trinity Church. Welcome to South Africa! I'm on vacation with my family right now, but I wanted to call to welcome you to Cape Town and say that we're looking forward to meeting you when we get back!" I couldn't believe it. What pastor took time out of his vacation to call a visiting college student? His kindness astounded me. My growing affection for South Africa and her people stretched even wider.

Liz prepared the most amazing meal, complete with ostrich, chutney, sweet butternut squash, avocado, and malva pudding—a rich, moist cake soaked in syrup and served warm with vanilla ice cream. All the food seemed far more exotic to me than typical West Michigan fare. The excitement and newness of it all heightened my senses. Colors appeared to be brighter, tastes richer, smells sweeter.

Nathan was on holiday in Zimbabwe for the week, so Jonathan took it upon himself to be my personal tour guide. He made it his mission to help me fall in love with his stomping grounds. It didn't take much. He was, as the national marketing campaign called it, Proudly South African—and rightly so. Though the stories he told in Michigan sounded too good to be true, I saw firsthand that he hadn't exaggerated Cape Town's beauty.

That first evening, while I could still feel reverberations of the aircraft engine underfoot, Jonathan whisked me off to the beach. The road curved out bravely along the coastline. I was shocked that people didn't drive right off the cliff while gawking at the view. We parked on the side of the road and ran across the street to Glen Beach—the place I'd seen those huge boulders protruding from the ocean during my aerial tour.

Jonathan jumped barefoot from rock to rock while I envied his agility and followed precariously in my unreliable flip-flops. I prayed I wouldn't slip and fracture an elbow on my first day in a foreign country. We found a decent perch on the brink of a rock and let our feet dangle toward the crashing waves. The same Lion's Head I'd seen in photos guarded our backs while the majestic peaks of the Twelve Apostles looked on from the coast. And if not for the Atlantic salt on my lips, it would've tasted just like a dream.

We sat just long enough for me to be entirely mesmerized by my surroundings, then turned to walk the strip of beachfront shops along the popular coastline of Camps Bay. Jonathan was barefoot the whole time—even inside the stores. I commented about America's "No Shirt, No Shoes, No Service" motto that I grew up on, and he just laughed it off—"This is Africa!" He handed coins to a cashier in exchange for some Chappies gum, and boasted that it cost mere pennies—nothing you could get in the States for that price. We sat in the sand, chewing our gum and drinking Schweppe's Granadilla out of glass bottles until the sun melted into the sea. In less than twelve hours, I was sold. South Africa had my heart.

During my first weeks in Cape Town, Gary and Liz graciously opened their home to me while I looked for more permanent accommodation. I had arrived during the break between college semesters and would start work when the campus reopened two weeks later. In the meantime, Jonathan, an avid surfer, took me to a different beach nearly every day. He and his friends were milking their winter holiday for all it was worth. They surfed, while I tried to shake myself out of what felt like a dream.

Besides playing tour guide, Jonathan accepted the monumental task of teaching me how to drive a manual transmission. I had purchased his sister's VW Jetta, but there was just one problem—I didn't know how to drive it. After a couple weeks of nightly practice, Jonathan declared me ready to hit the road. His dad, Gary, bravely placed his life in my hands and accompanied me on my first excursion onto a South African highway. Even though I'd been driving an automatic for five years, I felt as if I was learning the rules of the road all over again. The passing lane was on the right instead of the left, and most exit ramps veered off to the left—the opposite of what I was used to at home. We survived my first highway experience, but my confidence was not yet ready to emerge from its protective cocoon.

Sadly, I didn't have time to wait around for it. Winter break came to an end, and it was time for me to start working at the Student YMCA on the Cape Technikon campus—which meant I actually had to get myself there. The first morning, I buckled my nerves into the driver's seat, took a deep breath, and exhaled a prayer for help. It was now or never. I could do this. My new boss, Stefan, knew of my apprehension and phoned me the night before. "Just call me if you get stuck. I'll come get you wherever you are."

With great pride I managed to get on and off the highway successfully during the morning rush hour—and even found the correct exit on my first try. Then I reached a four-way stop. On an incline. Hill starts were not my forte. The brake lights of at least six cars shone in front of me before I could turn right. The line moved slowly until I rolled to a full stop, with three cars still ahead of me.

And I stalled my car.

I turned the key in the ignition. The engine sputtered but wouldn't turn over. I tried again. And again. Cars behind me started honking (or rather "hooting" as they say in South Africa). My face flushed while my engine flooded. I was stuck.

Suddenly a man appeared out of nowhere. He tapped my window, motioning me to open it. After hearing about the high crime rate in South Africa, for all I knew, the strange man was trying to steal my car. I cranked my window open a sliver and heard him rattling off words—in a different language. I replied in my mother tongue until a second man came along and told me (in English) that he and the other guy were going to push me through the intersection.

With their help, my stubborn little Jetta and I reached the end of the hill, rolling in neutral . . . until the pavement inclined as I turned into the Cape Technikon parking lot. All momentum petered out, smack in the middle of the entrance. I laughed, relieved that I had arrived. Mostly.

I reached for my cell phone and dialed Stefan's number. "Where are you?" he answered in a panic.

"I'm here," I replied.

"Oh. Well, good! C'mon up, then!"

"Uhh ... well ... My car isn't exactly in a parking spot yet. Could you come down and help me?"

We laughed for weeks about my grand entrance into campus ministry.

I followed Stefan up three flights of stairs to the Student YMCA, which occupied two small rooms in the bustling Student Center. The coffee bar that Stefan had described in his emails was actually just a single room with conference chairs lining three of the four walls. Against the fourth wall stood a plastic table with an electric kettle and four tins holding instant coffee, Rooibos tea, Ceylon tea, and sugar. Two plastic basins sat next to the kettle—one with dirty dishes and cold, soapy water, the other with clean water for rinsing. A brown mini-fridge hid below the table, chilling the milk. Stefan gestured to the open door next to the table. "This is my office," he explained, as I poked my head into the narrow, closet-like space.

"And this will be your office," Stefan announced, turning the handle on the door next to the coffee bar. "Well, yours and Kagiso's," he laughed. As the door opened, students crowded around from behind, awaiting my reaction. Across the middle of the room, a long strip of masking tape lined the floor. I squatted down to read the words scrawled across the tape in red marker: Anti-Kagiso Force Field. Arrows pointed away from one desk, toward the other. Stefan, the students, and I laughed in unison. "They thought you might need some protection against Kagiso's vibrant personality. He's a little . . . *loud*. He's at an evangelism course this week, so you have some time to settle in without him, but you'll meet him on Monday."

More surprising than the masking tape or the coffee bar was the view. The windows boasted a full, picture-perfect view of Table Mountain. I couldn't pull my eyes away.

Before going on vacation, Pastor Alan had arranged for two single ladies from Holy Trinity to spend time with me. Carin and Anja picked me up the next Saturday morning for a hike up Lion's Head.

The climb was incredible. A gravel path wound around the mountain to a breathtaking view from every angle. The Atlantic spanned without end. Opposite the ocean, the majesty of the city bowl spread out before us—buildings and roads, beaches and forests. We laughed and talked, breathless at times from the hike. I learned that Anja and Carin both came from Afrikaans families. "In South Africa, there are two types of white people," Carin explained. "English and Afrikaans. The Afrikaans culture originates from Dutch settlers who first landed in South Africa in 1652. Our language is actually quite similar to Dutch. English-speaking South Africans trace their history to British settlers who came in the late eighteenth and early nineteenth centuries."

It helped that Carin had spent several months in the States as an au pair. "If you say peanut butter and jelly here, people will look at you funny," she warned. "In South Africa, jelly is America's Jell-O, and jam here is what you call jelly. Your version of pancakes are crumpets here. If you order pancakes, you'll get flat crepes rolled up with filling inside." I made mental notes, wondering how much my brain would remember.

Within a week, Carin invited me to share her two-bedroom flat. I immediately agreed to move in. My first time living in an actual apartment other than on a college campus or in a homeless shelter, I felt more grown up than ever. It took a while to get used to the tight security—the burglar bars that made each window look like it belonged in a prison cell, the multiple locks and gates on every door. But Carin proved to be the ideal bridge for my transition. She graciously answered all my questions, like "Where do I go to buy postage stamps?" and "What's Marmite?" and "What are *rootis*?" With patience and a fair dose of laughter, she gradually chipped away at my ignorance.

Despite my enthrallment with South Africa and her people, Cape Town's moody temperature swings didn't impress me. Glorious beach days teased just before a string of bitter cold. Like, *really cold.* Back in the States, Nathan and Jonathan had warned me about Cape Town's frigid winters, but I'd argued, "How cold can it get? I mean . . . it's *Africa.* I'm from *Michigan.*" Ignoring their advice, I had packed a lightweight windbreaker, one hooded sweatshirt, and a couple of long-sleeve shirts, sure I'd be fine. I was wrong.

I called my mom. "Mom, I can see my breath in my bedroom! There is something wrong with this picture!"

I learned very quickly that buildings in South Africa didn't have central heating. No furnaces. No thermostats. Just space heaters and the occasional wood fireplace. If it was fifty-two degrees Fahrenheit outside, it was even colder inside. At night I slept with a T-shirt, long-sleeve shirt, my only hooded sweatshirt, and about four blankets, and still my nose felt like an ice cube.

Eventually, Carin took me shopping to buy a sweater. I hadn't even been in Cape Town long enough to know where I could get one. Store names like Pep, Edgars, and Mr. Price meant nothing to me. My former feelings of grown-up pride and independence quickly diminished into feeling like a little kid who needed Mommy to take her shopping for clothes.

After stepping out of her sky-blue hatchback at one of the stores, Carin suddenly yelled, *"Ag, nee!"*

"What's wrong?" I asked, mildly panicked.

"I just locked my keys in the car!" Presuming we would have to call a locksmith, I watched as Carin walked half a block down the street to a construction site, where several workers were building a new block of flats. She called out in a loud voice, "Excuse me! I've just locked my keys in my car. Could anyone help me?"

A flurry of volunteers piped up, "Oh sure, no problem!" Three burly guys in hard hats sauntered over to her car. In no time, they had bent the end of a wire into a hook, slipped it down between the window and door, and unhinged the lock device. Just like that. "Oh my gosh," I exclaimed. "That would *never* happen in my hometown! What's the point of locking the car at all if it's so easy to open?" Carin just laughed, thanked the construction workers, and retrieved the keys from her car.

Even though Alan and I emailed before my arrival, I was surprised by what I found at Holy Trinity's worship services. I never expected to see some of the same songs projected on the screen that I was used to singing at home. I didn't expect my theology to be so perfectly aligned with that of a church halfway around the world. And I certainly didn't expect to find Holy Trinity sending their own missionaries from Cape Town to other parts of the world.

I felt ashamed for thinking I was the super-spiritual missionary, fresh from Bible college, my head puffed up with knowledge. Truly God was building His kingdom from every tongue, tribe, and nation (Rev. 5:9). His body spanned every continent. The common bonds I shared with the Holy Trinity congregation made the church feel like family almost immediately.

After my first evening service, a new friend named Genevieve grabbed my arm and announced, "Come with me! Let's go find Kagiso so I can introduce you. He finished his evangelism course, so you'll start working with him tomorrow." I followed Genevieve into the tea room, where she tracked down a guy with brown skin, black, shoulder-length dreadlocks, and a bright, contagious smile. He shook my hand, cracked a joke, laughed loudly, and promised to see me at work the next day.

On Tuesday that week, I showed up at the Bible Institute to find Kagiso seated in the back of my Christian Ethics class. "Hey! What are you doing here?" he asked loudly, but in jest. "I thought I left you at Cape Tech!" I laughed, mostly relieved to see a familiar face. Between church on Sundays, sharing an office at the YMCA on Mondays, Wednesdays, and Fridays, and occupying the same lecture halls on Tuesdays and Thursdays, Kagiso was convinced I had ulterior motives. "Stop stalking me!" he teased.

"Hey now," I countered. "All the arrangements for my five months here were made *for* me, before I even landed in this country. How was I supposed to know we'd be sharing classes, an office, *and* a church?"

In the last week of July, three weeks after I'd left home, my mom called with a huge surprise. "Guess what?!" she exclaimed through the receiver. "I'm coming to visit you! I used my tax return money to buy a plane ticket. I'm landing next week, just in time to celebrate your twenty-first birthday!"

When Mom landed, I gave her no chance to recover from jet lag. In the span of seven days, we made the rounds. I took her to the YMCA and introduced her to Stefan, Kagiso, and numerous students. She met Alan, his family, and the congregation at Holy Trinity. She sat in my classes at the Bible Institute. Afterward, we drove to Cape Point, a popular nature reserve and tourist destination. We snapped photographs of ostriches stepping through fynbos and cheeky baboons perched atop parked cars. The curious African penguins at Boulders Beach greeted us before waddling through the sand to the salty sea.

We strolled stone paths in the inimitable Kirstenbosch Botanical Gardens, *oohing* and *ahhing* over protea, birds of paradise, and silverbush. The Table Mountain cable car carried us to the top of the landmark, where the panoramic views and cold winds were equally breathtaking. We drove along Chapman's Peak Drive, a glorious, bendy road boasting lengthy coastal scenery. Mom made me stop the car every few minutes so she could take more pictures.

One evening, Stefan invited Mom and me to his home for dinner. Kagiso and Stefan both lived about half an hour out of the city in the same direction, so I offered to give Kagiso a ride home so he wouldn't have to wait for the train. When we arrived at his house to drop him off, my mom got to meet his mom and brother, as well as Kagiso's grandfather, who was visiting for several weeks from his hometown of Kimberley, about nine hours away.

For my birthday, I arrived at the YMCA to find the entire coffee bar decorated with streamers, balloons, and three different cakes baked and decorated by separate individuals. That evening, Mom and I snuck off to Camps Bay beach for dinner and dessert. We lapped up chocolate gelato as waves lapped the shore. Contentment rode on the cusp of the breeze, and all was right in the world.

The honeymoon stage took a long time to wear off. I was enthralled with the beauty that caught my breath around every corner. The colors, the sounds, the stories. I had seen the colors of India, smelled its aromas, held its stories in the palm of my hand—but they hadn't wrapped themselves around my shoulders the way South Africa did. The intonations of the multiple languages I heard each day captivated me. The cultural nuances, the facial expressions, the songs. Oh, the songs. I never wanted them to end. At weekend camps, the students could sing for hours, swaying back and forth in the most beautiful harmonies. Songs that told stories of oppression and God's deliverance. Of perseverance in the midst of hardship. Of redemption. Translated lyrics on the projector screen taught me Sesotho words and isiXhosa phrases. The gift of worshipping in another language was almost too much for my heart to hold.

When I met her, the rainbow nation was a mere eight years old in her democracy. Elected to the presidency in 1994, Nelson Mandela led the country for five years before passing the baton to his comrade and vice president, Thabo Mbeki, in 1999. Though she was healing, South Africa not only bore untold scars from her past, many of the wounds were still scabbing over. She walked slowly, hunched over in recovery, the stitches of her incision not yet dissolved. The slowness was to be expected, after lying split wide open for generations in a state of segregation. Her body had been separated by those in authority, and now she had to get reacquainted with herself.

The most obvious scars showed themselves structurally—the jagged dissonance between multi-million-rand homes on the coast and piled up shacks in the waste-lands. Between 1960 and 1983, apartheid supporters shoved over three and a half million nonwhite South Africans out of their homes and herded them to designated neighborhoods according to skin color. Since then, the ramifications of these forced removals have resisted any attempts of undoing. Pockets of government housing have popped up here and there in an attempt to offer more suitable accommodation—basic brick homes with proper roofs and running water. A step up from corrugated metal, cardboard, and black bags, but still. The concrete pilings of apartheid may never be unearthed.

Less obvious were the wounds inside. Placing a bandage over an eyesore was one thing, but stopping the internal bleeding was a far greater challenge. It was also easier to ignore. Symptoms appeared when Themba, a student leader at the YMCA, called a familiar campsite asking for a reservation for one of our retreats. Upon hearing his thick Xhosa accent, the white person on the other end replied abruptly, "We're fully booked."

Stefan was furious. "*What?* That's ridiculous. They've never turned us down before. Pass me the phone." Stefan dialed the same number less than two minutes after Themba hung up. "How can I help you?" the original voice asked, soaked with pleasantry.

With his Afrikaaner accent, Stefan gave the dates of our camp and the number of beds we needed. The woman answered cheerily, "Of course, sir. We'd be happy to book that for you."

Sadly, it wasn't the only time I witnessed such blatant prejudice. On another occasion, some Xhosa girls from the YMCA were trying to find accommodation off campus. They scoured classified ads, calling number after number with no success. A white volunteer picked up the receiver and dialed a phone number the girls had already tried. The landlord asked outright: "Is the accommodation needed for you, or for someone else?"

"I'm calling on behalf of a friend," the volunteer replied.

"Is your friend black?"

"Yes."

"Sorry." *Click.*

The girls in search of a flat simply drew an *X* over that box in the classifieds and moved on to the next one. Stoic and undaunted. Calloused by a lifetime of ill treatment, yet determined to move on. My blood boiled at the injustice. Their resilience and perseverance reflected the strength of most black South African women I met. Theirs was not a superficial strength—it was anchored deep within, rooted in something far beyond themselves.

But not every interaction between culture groups was disheartening. In the places of South Africa where the body of Christ dwelled, I saw hope of wholeness. Places like the YMCA coffee bar and the tea room at Holy Trinity, where every tribe and tongue laughed and learned and loved together. The way it should be. And the way it would be soon.

CHAPTER 10

KAGISO

"I found him whom my soul loves."

—Song of Solomon 3:4 ESV

In those first few months, I didn't miss home much. I was too busy hiking trails, watching new friends surf the waves at Witsands Beach, and scattering guinea fowl at the sprawling Kirstenbosch Botanical Gardens. I was preoccupied talking theology on campus and spotting whales in False Bay from the Bible Institute cafeteria window. Too busy snapping photos of the white tablecloth cloud that mysteriously disintegrated after spilling over the brink of Table Mountain. Cape Town hadn't replaced home in my heart, but she filled me enough to distract me from the holes.

Cape Town entranced me with her beauty, warmth, and rich diversity. She pulled me under her spell. Five months with her wouldn't be enough to break the magic. Thinking about leaving made my stomach catch. By September, I'd made up my mind. I wanted to stay longer. I applied to extend my study permit for another two years and planned to pursue an honours degree at the Bible Institute—a one-year program between a bachelor's and master's degree. By attending classes part-time, I could stretch the course over two years to stay longer if I wanted. At first it wasn't a full jump into the pool—it was more of a swinging of the legs over the edge to test the temperature of the water. After all, I didn't *have* to stay the full two years. I just wanted to keep my options open. I already had airfare to Michigan to be home in time for Thanksgiving. But when my visa application got approved, I took a deep breath and booked another plane ticket back to Cape Town for four months later, in January 2003.

Soon after the renewal of my study permit, I began to realize just how much I enjoyed spending time with Kagiso. His natural ability to teach the Bible impressed me. He possessed an innate gift for engaging people of all types—male and female, black and white, young and old, extrovert and introvert. He drew students in with his contagious, charismatic personality. I looked forward to the days when we drove an hour together in peak traffic from Bible college in Kalk Bay to the train station near my flat in Rondebosch. We easily filled the time discussing topics from our Christian Ethics class, debating everything from euthanasia to birth control. Often, when Kagiso would ask me a question, he'd laugh at my answer. "What's so funny?" I'd ask, feeling self-conscious. "Nothing," he'd reply with a smile.

Between traffic lights we shared family backgrounds and future dreams. He told me about Mafikeng, the town where he grew up. His eyes brightened when he shared his dream to return one day to plant a church and a school there. "Cape Town has at least three Bible colleges and tons of Bible-teaching churches," he said. "Mafikeng has neither. I'm planning to go back to do ministry there. Maybe I'll plant a church first and then a school, or maybe the school will be the open door I need to start a church. I don't know the order yet, but they'll feed into each other, and then I'll start a campus ministry like the YMCA, which will pour into the church as well. All three ministries will be connected and can support one another." As a girl who doesn't think very far past what's for dinner, I admired his long-term plan to advance the kingdom.

A pang of shock coursed through me when I learned that his dad died when Kagiso was only seven years old. "What happened?"

"Motorcycle crash."

I gasped. Then, before I could recover from the news, he added, "My mom was seven months pregnant with my brother at the time."

"No!" I couldn't handle it. "Oh my gosh! I'm so sorry! That's terrible!"

Kagiso let out a laugh in response to my reaction. The steadiness and resilience in his voice as he recounted the tragedy proved that he could withstand the darkest of storms. I stood in awe of Kagiso's dedication, both to his family and to his work. After his dad died, he quickly rose up as the man of the house, accepting responsibilities like mowing the lawn, washing the floors, and looking after his brother. He graduated with a teaching degree, worked as a college lecturer for three years, and then decided to pursue ministry. When I met him, he was working at the Student YMCA three days a week. On the other two days, he spent two hours each way on the train to and from Bible College. His life was not easy, yet I never heard him complain.

He spoke six languages and had better people skills than I'd ever seen. Every day, I was more taken with his character and lively personality. Kagiso was a born leader, confident in his beliefs and his God's power. He could take any crowd and pull them together into meaningful conversation. He drew outsiders in, skillfully tugging those on the fringes until they were grafted into the fold. He made people feel noticed. He knew people mattered to God, so they mattered to him.

Because we were together so often, friends started dropping hints, wondering subtly and not so subtly whether we were becoming more than just colleagues and classmates. We brushed off all accusations, even as my face flushed at every mention. One weekend, Kagiso asked for volunteers to help paint the exterior of his mom's house. I turned down a day-trip invitation from Carin in favor of helping Kagiso and his mom. I showed up as the only female among a horde of able-bodied men, ready to paint. "You even make up excuses to see me on Saturdays too!" Kagiso joked. I couldn't argue.

At the time, Kagiso's grandfather was visiting from his hometown of Kimberley, nine hours from Cape Town. He sat silent on a wooden folding chair shaded by the only tree in the yard. Eyes masked by dark sunglasses, he looked on as we labored in the sun to transform the house's outside walls into a mustard gold. Months later, the story came out: At some point on that hot afternoon, Grandpa pointed a wagging finger at Kagiso and me and muttered to Kagiso's mom, "You watch those two."

One September afternoon, Kagiso asked if we could chat in the Bible Institute cafeteria. My pulse pounded in anticipation. *What could he want to talk about?* We stood in a corner by a wall of windows overlooking the waves as they splashed against the rocks bordering False Bay.

I waited for him to start.

"You know, we've been spending a lot of time together."

I nodded, my heart skipping every third beat.

"Since we work together in ministry, we really need to make sure that people don't get the wrong idea."

His words stomped the hopeful butterflies in my stomach to a quick death.

"Yeah. Of course. I completely agree." Inside, I knew it was the right choice, but disappointment was right there with me. I kept a smile on my face as I watched my hopes dash against the boulders with the waves outside.

Stop it, I scolded myself. *Stop thinking this way. You cannot be attracted to him. You came to this country to do ministry, not start a relationship.* I convinced myself that a romantic interest would detract from my ability to do the work God had prepared for me. A boyfriend would distract me and hamper my usefulness for the kingdom.

The cafeteria conversation didn't last long. We agreed to be more diligent in making sure we didn't behave in a way that raised any eyebrows. In the meantime, we still saw each other six or seven days a week, working side by side in various capacities. And without trying, Kagiso kept giving me more reasons to fall for him.

A couple weeks later, on the first of October, I drove Kagiso home after an evening Bible study on campus. When I parked in his mom's driveway, he didn't open the car door.

"You won't believe what Liz asked me the other day," he blurted. Before I could guess, he went on. "She asked if there's something going on between us."

I laughed. "Ha! She asked me the same thing."

"She did? She asked you too?" Now Kagiso was laughing. "I wonder why—what do you think made her ask both of us the same question?"

I shrugged in the dark. "I don't know. Maybe it's just because she sees us together so often."

"Well,"—he paused—"is she right? Is there something going on?"

Blood rushed to my cheeks. I didn't know what to say. "I don't know . . . is there?"

Right then and there we had *the conversation*. It was the first real confirmation I got that he had any interest in me whatsoever.

"Remember that day you asked me why I kept laughing at every answer you gave in the car?" Kagiso asked.

I nodded.

"I was laughing because you kept stealing my answers. Everything you said matched my own thoughts perfectly." After pausing, he asked, "Can you see yourself staying in South Africa . . . indefinitely?" I saw him testing the waters, wondering whether it was safe to step off the dock. At the time, he couldn't imagine living in the States for an extended period.

As much as I loved my home in Holland and knew I would miss it terribly, a deeper conviction said, "Yes. I want to stay." The rush of emotion made it hard to discern whether my desire stemmed from God or hormones.

The word *marriage* came up. It wasn't a proposal, but it wasn't a "hey, let's just date and see if it goes anywhere," either. It was more like, "I like you. You have the qualities I want in a spouse. If you feel the same, let's start a relationship with the view of working toward marriage."

Kagiso continued, "Because my dad's not around, I have a responsibility to look after my mom and brother. I've worked it out, and to keep my current commitments, I probably won't be able to get married for at least two years." My mind reeled. *Are we really having this conversation? I thought we were trying not to let this happen!*

It was nothing like I'd experienced in previous relationships, where the consensus was just to hang out and see what happened. Kagiso wasn't afraid of commitment. His straightforwardness and clear communication of motives and direction was even unusual for typical South Africans—and yet it felt right.

I was equal parts giddy and shocked. I wondered if maybe it *was* possible to continue mission work *and* be in a relationship. Perhaps the two weren't mutually exclusive. I drove home with a smile plastered across my face. When I got back to my flat, I called my mom right away, grateful that the time difference was in my favor. "I met the man I'm going to marry!" I announced without preface.

"What?! Who?!"

"Kagiso!"

Mom exhaled a quick sigh of relief. "Really?" She laughed. "Well, at least I've met him! And his mom and brother! And his grandpa!"

For weeks after our hefty conversation, schoolgirl giddiness danced with the wonder of new love until one day the music stopped and the sudden fluorescent lights of reality blinded me. Because of his passion for South Africa to be impacted by the gospel, a decision to marry Kagiso would mean pledging my allegiance not only to him and his family, but to his ministry and his country.

The weight of my commitment to stay in South Africa plummeted to the pit of my stomach and landed with a thunderous crash. I spent a whole evening sprawled on the carpet of my flat, sobbing over all that I would miss in America. Baby showers. Weddings. Birthdays. If Kagiso proposed and I said yes, I would be giving up home as I knew it. No more turkey dinners in November. No more white Christmases. No more spontaneous trips to Target or Chinese buffets with my sister.

I felt home slipping through my fingers once again, the great divide that mirrored my parents' divorce. Except this time, instead of splitting myself across town, I would be torn across the Atlantic. Funny how a potential marriage and a decades-old divorce could evoke the same emotion. I cried until I could cry no more, weeping over all I would be sacrificing by dedicating my life to this country, this people, this land that disappeared into oceans stretching to the ends of the earth.

By choosing missions and a cross-continental marriage, I was choosing a life untethered to home. I wondered whether it was worth it. I knew the Scripture passage where God promised that "everyone who has left houses or brothers or sisters or father or mother or children or fields for my sake will receive a hundred times as much and will inherit eternal life" (Matt. 19:29)—but at the time, I didn't care. I wanted *my* family and *my* home.

Then for a moment, the cloud cover lifted, and I could see the cross.

> But whatever was to my profit I now consider loss for the sake of Christ. What is more, I consider everything a loss compared to the surpassing greatness of knowing Christ Jesus my Lord, for whose sake I have lost all things. I consider them rubbish, that I may gain Christ and be found in him. (Philippians 3:7–9)

My so-called sacrifice was *nothing* compared to the sacrifice of Christ. Nothing at all.

The thought of being with Kagiso and serving alongside him in cross-cultural ministry dulled my heartache. Yes, there would be sadness and holes that could never be filled—but for the moment, the brightness on the horizon made everything else pale in comparison.

CHAPTER 11

CANCER

"Whom have I in heaven but you? And there is nothing on earth that I desire besides you. My flesh and my heart may fail, but God is the strength of my heart and my portion forever."

—Psalm 73:25–26 ESV

My first four months in South Africa passed in a blink. I flipped the calendar page to November and eyed my empty suitcases, the taste of turkey and stuffing taunting me. Before flying back to Michigan for Thanksgiving and Christmas, a college friend called with a huge surprise—she had raised enough money for Kagiso to visit the States. She wanted him to meet the rest of my family and see my hometown before we tied the knot.

That November, it was easy to leave Cape Town. Not only did I know I'd be back in January, I knew Kagiso would follow me just after Christmas. I couldn't wait to share stories and pictures in person with friends and family back home. The thought of introducing Kagiso to so many of the people and places that shaped me felt like a dream come true.

I hugged my mom and Sarah long and hard in the Grand Rapids airport, grateful beyond words to be reunited. Despite the many cultural adjustments, missing family remained the hardest part of being away. Back in Michigan, reverse culture shock slapped me in the face. Endless choices and blatant materialism bombarded me. One afternoon, Mom sent me to the store to buy rice. I stood in the aisle paralyzed by all the options—instant rice, five-minute rice, fifteen-minute rice, jasmine, long-grain, basmati. Wild rice and Spanish rice. In Cape Town, there were two options: white rice or brown. In Holland, my eyes scanned back and forth over shelf upon shelf until they brimmed with tears, overwhelmed. I grabbed a bag without reading the label and left the store just in time to evade a complete breakdown.

Sleeping in my own bed again made me think I'd never left. Mom hadn't changed a thing in my room. I curled up under my plaid duvet cover and smiled at the familiar digital clock on my twenty-year-old bedside table.

Holidays at home seemed sweeter after being away. I stuffed myself with turkey, mashed potatoes, and gravy on Thanksgiving. The next day, Mom, Sarah, and I trekked out to the Christmas tree farm to choose and cut the perfect blue spruce. Tradition continued as if no time had lapsed. We dipped steak and chicken into the spattering oil of the fondue pot on Christmas Eve, forgetting which sticks belonged to whom, like we did every year.

Just after Christmas, Kagiso boarded a plane in Cape Town—his first ever international flight. Across phone lines, I clucked over him like a mother hen: "Now, when you get to New York, you're going to have to change airports. Just ask someone how to get to the shuttle, and go straight from JFK to LaGuardia. Then find your gate and stay there until it's time to board."

Kagiso scoffed. "Are you kidding? I have six hours in New York! I'm not going to spend them in an airport; I'm going to explore! Times Square, Central Park . . ."

"No!" I pleaded. "You'll get lost and miss your flight!"

He just laughed and told me, "I'm an African. Africans don't get lost."

Shortly after his flight from Europe to New York landed, Mom's landline rang. "I made it," Kagiso announced from the baggage claim area at JFK. "I'm going to Times Square!"

I couldn't persuade him otherwise. Less than two hours later, the phone rang again. "What happened?" I asked.

"It's *freezing*! I got off at a bus stop and couldn't feel my face. I had to walk into a store just to get the feeling back."

"Where are you?"

"At LaGuardia."

I laughed. "Already?"

"Yeah, I'm not staying out there! It's *cold*!"

Still chuckling, I asked, "Well, what do you think of America so far?"

"It's huge! Everything's huge! The buildings are huge, the cars are huge, the people are huge . . ." His voice was swallowed by a wave of my own laughter.

"Well, I'm glad you made it to the right airport in time. Just one more flight. I'll see you soon."

Having Kagiso with me in Holland felt strange. Five months earlier, I was showing off Cape Town to my mom. The sweeping coastal city had seemed so glamorous with her wispy clouds and salty breezes. In the dead of winter, my hometown had little to boast about. The trees were bare, the icy roads precarious, the winds bitter. In hindsight, it was the worst season for Kagiso to visit. No tulips on display, no hot sand at Tunnel Park, no changing autumn leaves. Just stark and bland. And *cold.*

In many ways, Kagiso appeared to be out of place. His face was the only dark one in my church congregation, apart from one or two adopted kids sitting next to their white parents. His dreadlocks fascinated people. Just like in Cape Town, he related well to everyone, but I could tell it was taking mental strain—much like the acrobatics my mind endured while transitioning to Africa. I slipped back into my comfort zone and forgot to use the British English he was accustomed to hearing in South Africa. I asked him to get things out of the trunk of the car instead of the boot. People looked at him funny when he asked for directions to the loo.

One evening, we invited my grandma over for dinner. Shortly before she was due to arrive, my mom called to me from her bedroom. "Honey, go shovel the path for Grandma so she doesn't slip coming into the house." I called back, "I'm not shoveling. We have a man in the house!" I bundled Kagiso up with a down jacket, wool hat, and fleece scarf until all I could see were his dark eyes. "Here you go," I announced, handing him the shovel and gently pushing him toward the open front door. "Have fun!"

Less than a minute passed before I heard his voice through the window. "What do I do with all the snow?" I looked out and saw that he had pushed the shovel in a straight line until the snow accumulated into a huge heap in front of him. It took me a while to stop laughing enough for him to understand my instructions: "Lift and throw!"

On New Year's Eve, I made Kagiso watch the Times Square ball drop on the TV in Mom's basement. After we listened to the crowds in New York City shout the countdown, "Three . . . two . . . one . . . Happy New Year!" Kagiso asked, "That's it? That's what we've been sitting here waiting for?" A far cry from the loud, jovial pulse of South African streets that he knew and loved.

The celebratory vibe of the holidays was short-lived. Just after New Year's, a single word snatched the excitement away: *Cancer.*

Mom went in for a regular mammogram and a suspicious spot appeared, so she went back for a follow-up test. Waiting for the results was agony. An appointment with the oncologist confirmed our fears: breast cancer.

I plunged headlong into a pit of panic. A million questions assaulted me: Would she die? Were the cancerous cells spreading even as she slept? Just how aggressive were they? Could they be stopped? The very fact that the cells were unseen made the disease even scarier. And all of this transpired during Kagiso's visit—not exactly the vacation we had in mind.

I felt as if the cancer was controlling us. As if it had a mind of its own. Sleep eluded me—and I wasn't even the patient. Nights became my silent enemy. Floating question marks taunted me as I shifted and squirmed between the sheets. I started to view doctors as though they were as omniscient as God himself. I asked them questions they had no way of knowing, like, "How much longer? Will she be cured? How many chemotherapy drugs are available before you run out of options?"

To make things worse, my departure date to fly back to Cape Town was drawing near. Indecision haunted me. *Stay* and *go* collided as they beat their wings in my chest— crazed birds trapped in my rib cage, desperate to break free.

I clung to resentment like a security blanket. How could God do this? Why did He even let Eve bite the fruit in the Garden of Eden in the first place? He could've stopped her right then and there. He could've kept His creation from plummeting into the brokenness of realities like divorce and cancer. But He hadn't.

After initial tests, a team of doctors launched Mom into a rigorous treatment plan: a surgical lumpectomy just after my scheduled January fourteenth departure, followed by three months of chemotherapy, then six weeks of radiation. The chemo treatments would be every other Friday afternoon, so Mom could have the weekend to recover before going back to work at school. Sarah was living at Hope College but would go home every weekend to take care of Mom.

Even though we seemed to have "a plan," nothing was certain.

My mom, who had given everything of herself for my sister and me, languished in perhaps her most vulnerable point of need.

And I was leaving.

I squeezed her extra hard at airport security, and I left. She and her cancer waved good-bye, but they somehow boarded the plane right along with me. I couldn't shake them off. Reason frayed at the edges until a long thread unraveled and dangled loose in hysteria. And just like in second grade, when I used to tuck myself into the coat closet of my classroom to cry, I made for a stall in the airport bathroom and sobbed. Just like in second grade, I feared I would come home and my mom would be gone.

Every day I doubted my decision to return to South Africa. I questioned my loyalty to my family, especially since Mom was a single mom. I was keenly aware of the burden I had heaved onto Sarah's shoulders as I left her to assume the lonely and emotional role of caretaker on top of her full load of college classes. Night after night I tossed and turned in bed, afraid I had made the wrong choice. The melody of fear got stuck on repeat, and I couldn't get it out of my head. It became a siren song to my soul, wooing me closer to the jagged edge of despair.

Mom endured months of treatment, including an operation, recovery, chemotherapy, side effects, hair loss, radiation . . . the works. I watched from afar, getting daily updates from Sarah and Mom via email, phone calls, and Skype. Every time the phone rang, my heart leaped into my throat for fear of more bad news. Sometimes I just closed the blinds of my mind to block out the pain and pretended my heart wasn't home to answer when grief knocked on the door.

The peace I'd felt before going home for the holidays gave way to anxiety. I needed God to realign my thinking, or I would go mad. I needed Him to tell me that worry wouldn't solve anything. That Satan was the father of lies, and fear of death stemmed from the enemy. I needed Him to open my eyes to the truth that even if death came, it wouldn't be the end. Instead, I turned my back on the living water flowing within and spent my days facedown, sipping sand in a wasteland. Terrified of a future without my mom.

I wasn't angry with God, I just felt . . . flat. Neutral. Disengaged. Worst of all, I felt hypocritical. I had moved to Cape Town with hopes of impacting lives with the gospel, and I couldn't even bring myself to pray. I was supposed to be leading girls' Bible studies and having one-on-one discipleship meetings with students, but I could barely open my Bible. Telling girls from the YMCA that they could trust God felt like a lie. The words came out of habit and routine, but my heart scoffed at them. My whole job description was to encourage students to grow in the Christian faith, yet my own growth fell stagnant. My twenty-one-year-old self tripped into a pool of spiritual and emotional lethargy. I spent all my energy treading water, going nowhere. I wanted to glimpse the end result, to know what on earth the Lord was doing through this painful trial. My heart echoed the frustration of Job:

> But if I go to the east, he is not there; if I go to the west, I do not find him. When he is at work in the north, I do not see him; when he turns to the south, I catch no glimpse of him (Job 23:8–9).

I couldn't see God. In my weakest moments, I wondered if trusting Christ was worth it. How could He allow such a faithful, God-fearing woman like my mom to experience this level of suffering? Did my faith even matter? My family suffered just the same as unbelievers, so what was the point? I knew God existed, but the benefits of being His follower blurred with the tears in my eyes.

As I teetered on the edge of doubt, I looked at people I knew who didn't have Jesus. I saw their emptiness. Their complete lack of hope. I couldn't help but compare them to my mom. Even though Mom may have feared the unknown, she was anchored by her trust in Christ. Not just on the surface, either. She possessed a deep-seated hope within, fully persuaded of her Lord's ability to keep her tucked in the palm of His hand. She was held.

When I considered my options—either continuing to trust Jesus even when it hurt or turning my back on Him—I knew I would rather be held. Even more, I'd rather know that my mom was safe in His grip, no matter what the cancer did to her. Jesus's words about His followers echoed in my mind: "I give them eternal life, and they shall never perish; no one can snatch them out of my hand" (John 10:28). Even if her body did waste away in this life, she would still be held. She would be safe. She would be home.

God reminded me of a conversation in the Bible when some of Jesus's followers had turned away from Him. Jesus asked His remaining disciples, "You don't want to leave too, do you?" Then Simon Peter answered Him, "Lord, to whom shall we go? You have the words of eternal life" (John 6:66–68). Peter's words sealed it for me. Even if I flirted with doubt, where else could I go? God was my only hope.

Deep down, I knew Jesus was the way, the truth, and the life (John 14:6). I knew He held power over life and death. Most importantly, I knew He was faithful. He promised that *all* things work together for the good of those who love Him (Rom. 8:28). All things. Even cancer.

But I needed Him to rescue my flailing faith and teach me through trials that nothing could separate me (or my mom, or anyone else) from His love—not even the vilest of cancer diagnoses.

When it felt like Mom was losing the battle, God used sermons at Holy Trinity and encouragement from church friends to remind me that in Christ, Mom was more than a conqueror (Rom. 8:37). Over time, the Lord slowly and patiently rubbed gentle truths into my aching soul. He soothed me by lifting my chin to see beyond my immediate circumstances. To see that ultimately, the victory is in Christ, not in the remission of cancer. He had to show me that He who is in me is greater than he who is in the world (1 John 4:4). That He who is in me is greater than cancer. I had to learn that just as God puts reins and limitations on Satan, He has the same power over disease. Even cancer roams on a leash. It may do significant damage, but it never spreads apart from His control.

One night, when the guilt from leaving my mom threatened to overwhelm me, the Lord whispered loud enough to penetrate the back of my mind: "You're not the only one who can take care of her. I've got this." And He did. He called in an army of saints to tend to my mom in the most extravagant ways—rides to appointments, Frosties from Wendy's during chemo treatments, boxes of fresh bread delivered to her door, home-cooked meals. The way God used His people to care for my mom was a comfort to me, but not a complete relief. Their presence only masked the truth I felt: I'd been a selfish, uncaring daughter who didn't show up when I should have been there.

CHAPTER 12

MARRIED

*"LORD, you have assigned me my portion
and my cup; you have made my lot secure.
The boundary lines have fallen for me in pleasant
places; surely I have a delightful inheritance."*

—Psalm 16:5–6

Throughout Mom's treatment and my spiritual slump, Kagiso personified patience. He comforted me with words of assurance, pulling me back from the edge of crazed worry by reminding me of God's truth. He let me cry when I needed to cry, which was often. Surprisingly, I didn't scare him off with my unpredictable, fragile emotions. He saw me in my lowest moments, and didn't bolt. Instead of scolding me when I confessed my apathy toward God and the Bible, he kept taking me back to church. Back to God's house. Back to worship. It was as if he knew I'd come around in the end. But he gave me the time I needed, never pushing for change sooner than I was ready.

Eventually, slowly, the dust settled and Mom, Sarah, and I started to rebuild the walls from the foundation up. It was a tedious process, the destruction of the cancer so complete. But brick by brick we stacked rows of normalcy, cemented with apprehensive trust. Still separated by a vast ocean and too many miles, Mom's energy and my spiritual fervor made a steady comeback. Her visits to the doctor and my visits to regret became less frequent. As talk of cancer showed up less often, so did my anxiety.

After several months, test results indicated that all the cancer was gone. We rejoiced and thanked the Lord—but at the back of our minds, the walls were still susceptible to future attack. Mom started a drug called tamoxifen, prescribed to post-cancer patients. The doctor said, "Take this for five years. If you're still cancer-free five years from now, you're in the clear." Mom's hair started to grow back, and so did our resolve to seek out a new semblance of normal.

Even when the dark cloud of cancer hung overhead, life moved on in the shadows below. Kagiso and I kept leading Bible studies, having conversations with new and familiar students, hosting weekend retreats, and attending our own classes at Bible college.

Since Kagiso still lived at his mom's house about thirty minutes out of the city, I saw his mom often. Never once did I sense that she wasn't accepting of my relationship with her son—in fact, quite the opposite. Every time I visited her home, she presented me with home-cooked food and heartfelt conversation. I loved watching her interact with Kagiso. They teased each other relentlessly with a freedom and openness I admired.

It only took a glance to see that Kagiso's mom had raised her boys well. Both boys were disciplined, hard-working, and respectful. They did their work without complaint, and they did it well. She instilled a strong work ethic in them—likely a spillover from the pride she took in her own house. She taught her boys how to be responsible, and she did it all on her own. Her strength of character inspired me.

Their house became my home away from home. I bonded with Kagiso's mom over the island in her kitchen. Two cultures, two backgrounds, united across a countertop. Cooking was her love language. Affection stirred in me as she stirred *mealie pap* and *tamati* gravy at the stove. She worked miracles in her kitchen, whipping up the most amazing meals with very few ingredients and with no evidence of mess in her kitchen. It was magic.

Whenever I visited, I took copious mental notes and sometimes even written ones. She graciously taught me her tricks. I probably asked her six times how to make *dombi*, a type of bread that bakes inside a pot on top of the stove. One night, I even called her from my flat while making it myself to ensure I was doing it right. She taught me the secret to stirring *pap* with a huge wooden spoon and lots of muscle, and how to make the spicy tomato gravy called *chakalaka*. How to spice *snoek*, how to deep fry *vetkoek*, and even how to make home-made *droewors*—dried meat far better than beef jerky. She spoiled me with *koeksisters*, malva pudding, and peppermint crisp fridge tart.

We talked recipes and watched cooking shows, and once in a while she called me on the phone to ask a baking question. I would hear the television in the background. "Kate," she'd begin. "Tell me . . . what is shortening? And what on earth is a stick of margarine?" I laughed and translated the American lingo. The Lord used the kitchen to unite us. Two women, two generations who grew up doing things very differently from each other. A bridge across cultures.

In March 2003, less than a year after my first arrival in South Africa, my dad and Angela came to visit for a week. I stayed with them in a rented, sea-facing apartment in Bantry Bay, with a full wall of picture windows that overlooked the Atlantic. We stood on the balcony and pointed to Robben Island as waves crashed against boulders below and salty air blew through our hair. At last, they could see for themselves that I wasn't exaggerating Cape Town's beauty.

We *braaied*—the South African version of American grilling—at Kagiso's house. As we sat together on the shaded *stoep* outdoors, we talked and laughed with Kagiso's mom and brother, plates piled high with *pap* and mutton and hearts piled high with contentment.

One evening, I picked up seven of the girls that I worked with at the YMCA and drove them to Dad and Angela's rental apartment. They came armed with pots and grocery bags full of ingredients. They took over the kitchen, singing in Xhosa as they chopped and spiced and stirred. After a couple of hours, they proudly revealed the finished product: cooked tripe and diced sheep intestines.

With one meal, my two homes collided. At least my dad and Angela could say they experienced Africa. In fact, they loved their time in Cape Town so much that Dad announced he was paying for Sarah to make the same trip the following year.

Since Kagiso and I saw each other six days a week, our courtship looked different from that of other couples. As we spent our lives among college students, we were very aware that people were watching how we interacted with one another, perhaps taking cues for future relationships of their own. Occasionally, we stole away for a walk down the street, maybe to get a five rand soft serve from McDonald's or a sausage roll from King Pie. Or maybe just to breathe the African air.

We were watched on our walks too. At the time, mixed race couples were not very common. We almost caused car accidents as drivers stared at us at length in their rearview mirrors, presumably trying to ascertain whether we were holding hands. Some were even so bold as to turn their heads completely around. We laughed every time, pushing stereotypes and long-held racial tensions well past their comfort zones.

We often drove to Kagiso's mom's house after work on Fridays to watch TV with his mom and brother. On Saturday afternoons, we worked on Bible college assignments together, spreading our church history timelines across his mom's carpet while she served us *polony* sandwiches cut into triangles and glasses of mango juice on fancy trays. Sundays we often hung out with church family or *braaied* at Kagiso's mom's house. Her serene back *stoep* demanded relaxation. I couldn't help but feel as if I'd been welcomed home.

In late October 2003, just over a year after we started dating, my mom's birthday rolled around. Kagiso knew I was missing her more than usual that day, so he suggested that we go to Kirstenbosch Botanical Gardens as a special treat. On the way there, Kagiso said, "I haven't called your mom to say happy birthday yet. I should do it now before she leaves for work." I'd learned in the past year that calling people on their birthdays was an important part of Kagiso's culture. People might not receive gifts or cards, but they were sure to get dozens of phone calls. Kagiso asked me to stop at a pay phone. Since I had already talked to her that day, I stayed in the car while he jumped out and dialed the four hundred digits required to make an international call from a pay phone using a prepaid calling card.

At Kirstenbosch, the weather was perfect. As we strolled along, we took in the scenery and the realization that I was leaving in three weeks to go back to Michigan for Thanksgiving and Christmas. We dragged our feet a bit, hoping if we lingered, the time we had together before my departure would last a little longer.

When we reached a stone path with a narrow, shallow stream, we stopped and sat on some large rocks on the bank. We took off our shoes and let our feet soak in the moment. Kagiso leaned over and gently ran his fingers through the cool water. He started talking about how much I meant to him, and how much our relationship had changed him for the better. I figured, *He's just sentimental because I'm leaving soon.*

Then, to my complete surprise, he reached his hand into the sand under the water, and pulled out a solitaire diamond ring! He shook off the dripping water, held it out to me, and asked, "Will you marry me?"

"Yes!" I exclaimed without hesitating. My heart pounded with excitement and shock. "How did you *do* that?" I asked, still in awe of the way he pulled the ring out of the sand. "And how long have you been planning this?"

In typical fashion, he just laughed and gave no real explanation to satisfy my queries. He did, however, reveal that he had ulterior motives when calling my mom for her birthday. "I asked for her permission to marry you, and she said yes." He then recounted a conversation he'd had with my dad ten months earlier, when Kagiso visited Michigan. Apparently my dad had pulled him aside one evening and said, "If you want to marry Kate, you don't have to ask me first. You can just do it."

On our way back to the car, Kagiso had to hold my hand to keep me from floating away. He teased me for the way I couldn't stop gawking over the sparkles in my ring. Back at my apartment, I called everyone I knew to share the news.

After some discussion, we decided to have two wedding ceremonies—one in Michigan, one in South Africa. That way, both sides of the family could be part of our celebration. We set dates for the following June and July—a summer wedding in Michigan and a winter wedding in Cape Town, two weeks apart.

When I left Kagiso at the airport in November, the separation didn't seem quite as unbearable—I had two weddings to plan, a mom in remission, and a fiancé waiting for me upon my return.

Shortly after the proposal, Kagiso's aunt, Mamadu, heard about our engagement and asked for our clothing measurements. A few months later, she came to visit Cape Town from Pretoria, armed with matching traditional South African outfits for Kagiso and me to wear at our reception. A neighbor friend of hers had handmade them just for us. The material was a bright sunflower gold accented with black. We tried them on, and they fit perfectly. As we modeled our attire for Kagiso's mom and aunt, it suddenly became real. I was getting married. In Africa.

A few months before our wedding, at age twenty-two, I said good-bye to my flat mate and moved into a tiny, single-roomed granny flat on a large plot of land south of the city—the equivalent of a bachelor's apartment or a nanny's quarters attached to a main house on a bigger property. The wide-open space was rare in Cape Town. In less than two years, I had grown accustomed to the noise and bustle of the crowded urban landscape.

During that final period of singleness, in March of 2004, Sarah cashed in her gifted plane ticket from Dad and Angela and came to visit me—her first trip to Africa, and our last hurrah as bachelorette sisters. I tried not to think too much about how our relationship might change after I became a wife. Instead, we talked late into the night, reminiscing and baking cookies with the Nestlé Toll House chocolate chips she brought—the taste of home.

Exactly two weeks after Kagiso and I spoke our vows in Michigan in June of 2004, we were back in Cape Town doing the same. I joked that not many girls got to wear their wedding dress twice. Fewer could boast of having a summer wedding and a winter wedding two weeks apart. Mom flew over with a dear friend to witness the lively occasion. That time, I didn't walk down the aisle, but stepped to the beat of vocalists harmonizing the Setswana lyrics, *"Tshwang, tshwang, tshwang . . ."* And the guests, they didn't stand stoic in the wooden pews. They charged me with jubilant enthusiasm, crowding me in with cell phones raised high to my face, snapping photos left and right. I could barely make my way through the thick mass to the front of the church.

Kagiso's relatives and friends made the trek from Kimberley, Johannesburg, Pretoria, and Mmabatho for the celebration. With multiple provinces and cultures represented, I glimpsed a preview of the wedding feast of the Lamb. While our friend preached, we laughed as Kagiso's uncle, Son, kept having to yank his two-year-old, Kabelo, from his attempts to climb the steps to the pulpit.

After the ceremony, we changed from the traditional white dress and black suit into our customary African attire—the wedding gift from Kagiso's aunt. As we stepped outside the church, our goldenrod yellow outfits shouted hope and life against a backdrop of gray winter clouds.

At the reception, South African music pumped from rented speakers and reverberated against the walls. The majestic gold of our post-wedding attire swayed happiness through the crowds as we danced and danced until the sub-Saharan beat slipped into my bloodstream and took over my pulse.

When it came time for the speeches, my mom stood, trembling but brave. Turning to the newly acquired branches of my family tree, she lifted the microphone to her lips.

"Take care of her," she said to the watching crowd, salty tears slipping down her cheeks. And they did. And they have. And they do. They have fed me and clothed me. Nourished me and sheltered me. Lifted me and held me. They have been Christ to me. They've grafted me in as one of their own, love flowing up from the very roots, buried deep in African soil.

The deejay cranked up the music again, and soon a conga line snaked through the rented gymnasium. Black and white, Afrikaans and Tswana, Xhosa and English, American and South African—we all linked shoulders and hips and bounced in awkward unison. A tangled cord of broken people, united by love.

As the conga line dissipated, a circle formed, and brave souls took turns jumping into the middle to show off their moves. Kagiso's uncle, Son, jived on the fringes in his sky-blue suit when he wasn't chasing two-year-old Kabelo across the open circle. I joined arms with my mom and brand-new mother-in-law. We made a chain with her sisters and danced together—a braided strand of yarn. Multiple colors interwoven as one. My husband's relatives spread open the afghan of their family and folded me in. They even gave me a new name, according to their custom—*Refilwe*, which means, "we have been given." They thought they'd been given a gift in me, but the truth was, I was the one who had been given much. So very much.

CHAPTER 13

CHANGE

"Change and decay in all around I see;
O Thou who changest not, abide with me."

—Henry Lyte, "Abide with Me"

After a gorgeous and relaxing honeymoon with stops in Green Point, Mossel Bay, and Robertson, we returned to our new abode to settle in as husband and wife. That first year, home was one room. As in, when we opened the front door, we could see the bed. We had to walk past the bed to get to the bathroom, which boasted the only other door in the whole place. The joke was that we could never have a proper married couple's fight, since the bathroom door was on a sliding track. If one of us wanted to slam a door in anger or frustration, the only options were to storm out the front door and end up outside, or attempt to slam the sliding bathroom door.

We purposely chose not to have a television—some of the best premarital advice we received. Living in a one-room cottage without TV or internet resulted in a lot of face-to-face communication in those early days. Sometimes the word count exceeded Kagiso's daily limit. I grew up in a house full of girls. Talking was pretty much all we did. All the time. Suddenly I found myself in close quarters with someone who didn't hold the same appreciation for yapping about nothing.

We shared one car, driving to and from work together three days a week and finishing up our respective degrees at Bible college the other two days. During this time, Kagiso started preaching occasionally at our church. Sermon preparation didn't come easily in the beginning. Each opportunity came with tedious, time-consuming labor. In the evenings after we got home from working a full day at the YMCA, Kagiso pored for hours over commentaries and computer screen, intently focused on his text. I, on the other hand, wanted to chat. I naïvely thought his evenings should be devoted to me. It took serious amounts of self-control to glue my lips shut for long periods of time so he could work. In those days, preaching weeks were few and far between, but they were lonely times for me. I stood silent, washing dishes at the kitchen sink, willing myself not to speak, wondering what it would be like if this became the norm.

The first couple months of our marriage, I fought a series of illnesses in quick succession—first a violent bout of stomach flu, then a severe kidney infection that kept me flat on my back for days. All I wanted was for my mom to hold my hair back while I leaned over the toilet. I wanted her to wipe a cold, wet washcloth across my forehead the way she always did when I threw up.

When I committed to living in South Africa, I knew I would miss many things about my life in the States—but I never anticipated that the way my mom held my hair back while I vomited would be one of them. It was one of many subtle expectations I didn't even know I had until it crept up and revealed itself. Sometimes a girl just wants her mom. But there I was, with this new spouse who knew nothing of holding hair or wiping foreheads. Neither he nor his mom ever threw up, nor did they have hair like mine that got in the way.

I wanted him to read my mind, to just know my needs and meet them without even having to be asked. Instead, he hovered over me, with no idea what to do. I had to be intentional about voicing my desires, making specific requests during my point of need. It was a shifting of dependency, a quiet acknowledgement that I was now bound to him, in sickness and in health. I may have wanted my mom, but she was thousands of miles away. Instead, my husband willingly stepped into position behind me as I knelt on the bathroom floor, washcloth in his hand, ready to hold my hair.

Making a home is synonymous with commitment. It's committing one's whole self to a place—both energy and affections. Marrying into a foreign country divided my affections. Like the effect of my parents' divorce, home was again split in half. I spent much of my time trying to weld the two halves together. Lining up the edges as best I could, I labored to make home whole again. My goal was to draw out the best pieces of each culture and mosaic them into something that resembled familiar. I filled my grocery cart with beloved Heinz ketchup, refusing to buy the more popular All Gold tomato sauce. I clung to certain American words like *ketchup*, but gave in to South African terms like *boot* instead of *trunk*, and *cooldrink* instead of *pop* or *soda*. I embraced South African tea drinking instead of the late-night coffee that carried me through college.

In preparation of my first December away from home, my mom sent a three-foot, artificial Christmas tree and a box of non-breakable ornaments. Kagiso rolled his eyes while I assembled the plastic limbs halfheartedly, longing for the scent of a freshly cut blue spruce. The tiny tree had no hope of emulating a Michigan Christmas, not when the sun in Cape Town didn't go down until well after nine p.m., and temperatures peaked above ninety degrees.

If only I could have seen that I was using the wrong template to create my new model of home. I was gluing into an earthly mold, not a heavenly one. I was still storing up treasures for myself that I could hold and see and smell (Matt. 6:19–21). Treasures that, because of their familiarity and tradition, made me feel grounded and secure. I thought that was what made a home. After all the homes I'd lost, I still thought I could keep some things the same. Even halfway around the world.

In November, four months after our honeymoon, I emerged from the miniature bathroom one Sunday morning with a new identity. White plastic stick in hand, the two pink stripes across the middle pronounced a significant life change—we were parents. I don't think I actually shed tears, but my state of shock produced a string of initial complaints: "We've only been married four months! I'm only twenty-three—too young to have a baby!" My godly husband quickly rebuked me: "Children are a blessing from the Lord. I think you should check your attitude and ask God to help you become grateful."

With pronounced stubbornness I sulked for a few more days, mostly just terrified of what lay ahead. I wasn't ready to be a mom yet. I thought having a child would confine me—limit me from being able to hang out with friends or continue in student ministry. I certainly hadn't adjusted to living in a foreign country, let alone my four-month-old title of "wife"—how could I also add "mother"? I missed my own mom terribly—how could I become one myself?

We couldn't get in to see a doctor until the following week to confirm the pregnancy. Those days before the appointment were long. We didn't want to share the news until we were sure, but I have never been fond of keeping secrets—and this was quite possibly the biggest secret I'd ever had to keep. When nobody was in the office at work, I snuck onto pregnancy websites, reading tips and advice about what to do and not do. I stopped drinking caffeine and started walking more gingerly, afraid a sudden movement might jeopardize the baby's development.

Finally, on the third Thursday of November 2004, I lay on the white paper atop the obstetrician's examining table—and we heard the heartbeat. I couldn't believe it. Life was growing inside of me. I stared at the obscure images on the black and white sonogram screen and wondered how anyone could possibly see what I was seeing and not believe there was a God. For the first time since I saw the positive test result, excitement and wonder coursed through me with the swishing noise of the ultrasound machine.

That same night, Kagiso and I graduated from the Bible Institute of South Africa—he with a hard-earned bachelor's degree and me with a post-graduate honours degree. I stood in the line of graduates that evening, keenly aware that my family was celebrating Thanksgiving Day in America without me, and I was wearing a cap and gown without them. We'd never been apart on Thanksgiving before, and they had never missed one of my graduation ceremonies. I felt an expanse widening between us, but I was helpless to stop it from growing. Just like the child in my womb. And yet I was quite possibly more grateful that Thanksgiving Day than I'd ever been.

CHAPTER 14

BIRTH

"How can I repay the LORD for all his goodness to me?"

—Psalm 116:12

Less than two months later, in January 2005, Kagiso and I were at a YMCA staff and student council retreat when his mom called with devastating news. Kagiso's uncle, Son, had passed away. His mom's brother. It was unthinkable. He had just been dancing at our wedding in Cape Town six months earlier, with his wife and two-year-old son, Kabelo. Full of life.

In a state of mild shock, we left our work retreat immediately to prepare for the nine-hour drive from Cape Town to Kimberley for the funeral. We rode with Kagiso's mom and brother, a blanket of sadness adding to the already oppressive summer heat. Kagiso and his mom maintained their composure but spent most of the ride without words. My first trimester nausea was in full force, magnified by the lengthy, hot road trip. I felt like a burden, gritting my teeth when I felt sick and crossing my legs when I had to pee. At long last, we arrived late at night at the family compound in the township of Galeshewe. Thick grief created an eerie silence on the property. All the furniture had been removed from the main sitting area inside the house. In its place, white plastic chairs lined the bare walls. Quiet mourners sat in a square, staring at the tile floor.

My heart broke for the family. For Kagiso, for his mom. I cried thinking about Kagiso's grandpa having lost a second son. My stomach churned at the thought of Kabelo growing up without a dad.

There's something about shared grief that binds affections. Roots spread and grow deeper, all tangled together in empathy. Through this unexpected loss, my love for the family I married into wrapped itself even tighter around the trunk of the family tree.

Galeshewe is far less developed than the suburbs of Cape Town. Though I had been there a few times, it was my first experience at a Batswana funeral. The next few days blurred in a flurry of activity. Countless spheres of preparation needed to be addressed. Family members dispersed to tackle the long list of responsibilities. Some dealt with obtaining a death certificate from Home Affairs and notifying life insurance and funeral policies, while others mobilized men to pitch a large tent to shade the front yard. Laundry had to be hand washed, rinsed, and hung on one of the three clotheslines slung across the backyard. Relatives scattered to Woolworth's and Edgars to purchase proper funeral attire.

Services would be held at the house every evening for the five consecutive nights leading up to the Saturday morning burial. On each evening, those in attendance would expect to be served tea and biscuits. Somebody had to stock up on tea bags, sugar, and milk. Someone else would have to bake the cookies. After the funeral, attendees would walk together from the cemetery back to the house, where they would share a home-cooked meal under the tent. Hundreds of people would need to be fed. Leading up to the funeral, all the family members filtering in and out of the house still needed to eat breakfast, lunch, and dinner. The household buzzed like a busy hive.

The morning after we arrived, I woke up and stepped outside to brush my teeth. The only water source at the house was a single faucet on the exterior wall, which emptied into a drain in the ground. To my left, a white pick-up truck had parked next to the house. Its open bed was packed full of live sheep, bleating in mass confusion. I turned to my right and watched as three men with unfamiliar faces labored to dig a deep pit next to the outhouse. Kagiso walked up and saw the question mark on my face.

"They're getting ready to slaughter the sheep," he explained. I nodded, holding my breath to avoid the smell, as he took my elbow and led me into the house for some breakfast. I sat in front of the television and ate buttered bread off a plastic plate to calm my pregnancy-induced nausea. I felt a bit out of place, as everyone else had tasks to fill their day. Kagiso had to drop off his mom at the grocery store before driving his uncle to the funeral parlor. "Just sit here and rest until I get back," he suggested. He knew the first trimester had made me more tired than usual. Through the open window, I watched Son's youngest boy, Kabelo. The carefree, rambunctious two-year-old had no idea what this occasion meant for his future.

About an hour later, I needed the bathroom. Before I could make it to the toilet outside, some of Kagiso's cousins greeted me, smiling. "Morning!" They sat in a row of chairs, with plastic trays on their laps. To my shock, on each tray was a sheep's head—eyes glazed over, limp tongue sticking out. The cousins each held a flat razor blade between their forefinger and thumb, skillfully shaving off the sheep's hair.

The odor was pungent. A wave of nausea swept over me. I returned the greeting and covered my mouth, rounding the corner of the house to escape the animals' stares and smells. Around the bend stood more cousins, elbows deep in huge metal bowls filled with sheep intestines. They spoke cheerful hellos as flies swarmed around the fold-up tables in front of them. Desperate for clean air, I kept walking until I found Kagiso's cousin, Naledi. Hand still covering my mouth, I said, "I have to get out of here." Just three months ahead of me in her first pregnancy, she understood. With part sympathy and part amusement, Naledi held my arm and guided me away from the dismembered animals back into the house. I never even got to use the toilet. Naledi led me back to the couch in front of the TV, then brought me some water and more plain bread to settle my stomach.

We didn't know it at the time, but Naledi and I both had girls growing in our wombs. That week, we bonded over cheese sandwiches in lieu of the meat that others kept offering. Both of us were averse to the smell of it—a new development that came with growing a baby.

Naledi took me under her wing and called me her sister. She took me shopping too. I learned that in their culture, pregnant women don't wear black to a funeral. As a sign of new life within, they're to wear any other color, often white. They also wear hats. We browsed store after store, stepping out of dressing rooms to model options and ask each other's opinions. We both found dresses we loved—mine, a white sleeveless V neck with brown flowers—then moved on to the next store to find coordinating sun hats and shoes. The whole concept of shopping before a funeral was new to me—yet because Naledi embraced me as her sister, I felt as though I belonged.

The whole family welcomed me with open arms. They loved me into their clan and culture as though I'd always been one of them. Traditionally, the newest bride in the family is the *makoti*, and the *makoti* is expected to fulfill certain expectations and responsibilities. According to the culture, she is to take up her new role in the home by cooking, cleaning, and washing dishes all day. She is often expected to dress in a certain way, usually with a skirt and headscarf. This was not my experience. Instead, my in-laws raised me up on a pedestal and served me, when I was supposed to be serving them. They made sure I was comfortable and well cared for. My mom-in-law and her sister lavished me with heaping plates of food and tall glasses of cold Fanta. They did their best to make sure I was never alone or feeling out of place. As often as they remembered, they switched the conversation to English so I wouldn't feel left out.

In hindsight, this special treatment could have caused a pronounced sense of division between "them" and "me," as I had felt on my mission trip to India. Instead, the way they went to great lengths to care for me made me feel accepted. I was one of them. They didn't care that I was the only white face in the neighborhood. In their minds, community crossed both culture and shade of skin. The smiles in their eyes told me that their home was my home.

On our first anniversary, in June 2005, I stood at the wooden gate at the end of our long driveway. One hand held my swollen abdomen while I unlatched the gate with the other. Our first child was due to be born in just over a month. A new chapter was a page turn away. We deemed our cute little granny flat too cramped to welcome a third person and began the search for alternate accommodation. As He always does, the Lord had a plan. Some American missionary friends who lectured at our Bible College asked us to house-sit their furnished home for a year while they went overseas on furlough. We accepted gratefully and packed our first year of memories into cardboard boxes.

I was surprised by how sad I was to leave that first abode. With deep sentimental attachment, I tore my heart from that place with its green pasture and sliding bathroom door. I'd heard it said that being a parent was like having your heart walk around outside of your body. Living cross-culturally and moving often was like leaving remnants of my heart everywhere I went.

In July 2005, we moved into the lecturers' home. Though we were spoiled and beyond grateful for the gorgeous provision, we were still living on top of another family's belongings. Like borrowing a friend's clothes that would soon need to be returned.

My mom came from Michigan for a six-week visit in anticipation of her first grandchild's birth. I hadn't seen her since our wedding a year earlier. Happy tears marked our reunion, especially when Mom wrapped her hands around all she could see of her grandbaby, still hidden away in my protruding belly. "You look so small!" Mom exclaimed. "Oh, I'm just so happy to be here, I can't even stand it!"

After months of failed attempts to get us to find out the gender of the baby, Mom arrived laden with suitcases full of pink and blue. "I'll just return everything else after we find out if it's a boy or a girl," she reasoned. It was so like her. She unpacked an entire baby-shower-by-mail, organized by dear friends back in Michigan. Their love that spanned an ocean meant so much to me. But instead of making me feel closer to home, the pang of distance grew sharper. My American friends wouldn't be able to cuddle my newborn. I had no idea when Sarah or my dad would get to meet the baby. I couldn't think about it for too long or the waves of sadness would swell to overwhelming heights.

Mom and I passed the time by strolling Fish Hoek beach with soft serve ice-cream cones in hand. We visited

Greenmarket Square and the V & A Waterfront Mall. I drove her to all the destinations that became her favorites on her first two visits—Cape Point, Chapman's Peak Drive, and Kirstenbosch Gardens. With each day, I waddled a little slower and grew more uncomfortable.

One Monday evening about two weeks after Mom arrived, we sat on the couch watching TV. Just before turning in for the night, we discussed our plans for the next day. "A trip to the grocery store might be about as much as I can handle," I joked.

"That's fine!" Mom said. "Let's just wait and see how you're feeling. We've done so much already. We can lay low tomorrow."

The next morning, I woke up around four o'clock with sharp stomach pains. I thought it was indigestion, so I got out of bed in search of relief. After enduring the discomfort for over an hour, I tapped Kagiso awake. "I think I might be in labor." He mumbled a sleepy, "Okay," rolled over, and carried on snoring.

I rolled my eyes and heaved my body around to try to sleep some more, but it hurt too much. "Kagiso, I really think I'm in labor," I prodded again. He stirred himself into a sitting position and decided we should take the advice of a doctor friend, who said if we wanted to test whether labor was false or not, we should take a walk. If the contractions persisted, it was probably genuine labor. So off we went in the early morning darkness, shuffling the sleeping streets of Fish Hoek in our bathrobes. We paused every few moments as I doubled over from the intensity of the contractions. We made the unified assumption that I was, in fact, in labor, and turned around. Back at the house, I insisted on washing my hair. Who knew how long it would be before I could wash my hair again? I woke my mom and she jumped up in a flurry of excitement. "Really? It's happening! Oh my gosh, okay! I'm ready!"

"Relax." I laughed. "I'm gonna take a shower first, then we can leave. You have time." I showered in spurts, stopping to hold the wall during contractions. Prenatal classes warned me I wouldn't be allowed to eat at the hospital during labor, so I stuffed my face with crackers in the back seat of the car as the sun peeked over the horizon.

In the labor ward, Kagiso maintained his post by my side while both my mom and his mom stood shoulder to shoulder at the foot of the bed. A perfect picture of two families becoming one. My two anchors of home clung to each other in shared anticipation. And my heart smiled at the Lord's kindness.

My labor was hard. The epidural I requested after five hours only numbed my right leg. A nurse advised me to lay on my left side so the drug might find its way to the unaffected part of my body, but that side hurt the most. At the twelve-hour mark, the doctor announced it was time to push. After several attempts, my obstetrician expressed concern that the baby's head hadn't dropped—it was still high up above my pelvic bone. With another push came meconium, evidence that the baby was in distress. The next moments blurred together and included the words "emergency Caesarean" as I was moved to a stretcher and hurried down the passage to an operating theatre. A nurse guided Kagiso to a separate room to change into sanitized scrubs. Both moms squeezed my hands as a hospital porter wheeled me away. I blinked back a few threatening tears and saw my mom wipe a tissue across her eyes. "We'll see you when you get out!" she called after me.

Several people in scrubs hustled about the cold, sterile room, while others stood on either side to prop me into an upright position, my right leg still completely numb. The flurry of activity and voices calling out medical terminology distracted me from my fear. I just wanted them to do what they had to do to get my baby out safely.

Nurses held my arms and instructed me to lean over a pillow while sitting on the edge of the operating table. From his position behind me, the anesthesiologist instructed, "Tell me when you feel another contraction."

I moaned and in the height of the pain, he injected a needle into my lower back. Within moments, everything went numb, all the way up to my neck. "Why didn't you do this twelve hours ago?" I joked. Nurses lowered me onto my back and wheeled me under a bright light. A thin sheet and the scent of disinfectant covered me. I glanced down as another nurse placed a fabric curtain-like barrier across my body, to block me from seeing anything below my chest.

Kagiso appeared at my head, decked out in sky-blue scrubs and a matching surgeon's cap, ready to watch. A voice offered him a stool on wheels. "You're going to want this," the voice insisted. "Oh no, I'm fine," Kagiso countered. The other voice was not so sure. "That's what all the dads say, right before they pass out. Some dads have missed the whole thing and ended up in their own hospital beds right next to their postpartum wives." Kagiso laughed the loud, contagious laugh I fell in love with three years earlier.

Abandoning the stool invitation, he turned to face me. His calm presence soothed me. "You okay?" he asked, stroking the surgical cap covering my hair.

"I'm freezing." My teeth chattered uncontrollably.

I turned my eyes toward the anesthesiologist standing behind me. "Is this normal? I'm really, really cold. I can't stop shivering." He eyed the nearby monitor and assured me I was fine.

"What's that?" Kagiso asked the obstetrician, leaning over the curtain for a better view. The doctor laughed, surprised by his interest. I felt strong tugs on my lower abdomen.

Then suddenly—a newborn baby's cry. Kagiso drew in an audible breath.

"It's a girl!" the doctor announced.

"It's a girl?" I repeated in disbelief, looking to my husband for confirmation. "Did he say 'girl'? Are you sure?"

Even though we hadn't found out in advance, I was convinced the baby was going to be a boy. Everybody thought so, for no reason other than a collective hunch. Everyone, that is, except my mom. She later confessed that as soon as she got off the plane in Cape Town and saw that I was carrying all tight and compact in the front, she guessed it was a girl. She said she had carried me and Sarah the same way. In the end, I learned that the reason I had to have an emergency Caesarean was the same reason my mom had an emergency operation with me. It turned out my pelvic bone was too narrow—apparently a trait that can be (and was, in this case) passed on genetically. Knowing I carried and delivered my firstborn in the same way my mom carried and delivered me made me feel a new bond with her. Mirroring her birth story gave purpose and meaning to my own.

As I lay on the operating table getting stitched up, Kagiso and I debated names. "I can't believe we're doing this now," I complained between chattering teeth, peeved that we couldn't agree before then. We'd decided on a boy's name before the contractions started, but still had a short list of three or four girls' names we were considering. Mom's only request was that it would be something Americans could pronounce. After some deliberation, we landed on a name: Dineo. In Setswana, it means "abundance of gifts." Indeed, in her, God blessed us with an abundance of gifts.

Becoming a mom in South Africa wrapped my identity tight around that far and foreign land. I became more than just a visiting volunteer missionary. I did more than marry a local. I brought forth life in the shade of that vast expanse. Giving birth on African soil gave me a sense of confidence—a sense of place. I suddenly had someone else to care for besides myself. Though my sweet girl was half American, she was just as much South African. She belonged—and through her, I felt that I did too. She held a birthright as a citizen of that beautiful rainbow nation—and as her guardian, I reasoned that I could claim the same protections by association.

I thought about Jesus's mother Mary, how she housed the Son of God in the fiber of her being. How the Father split her body open in the darkness of night to let out the light of the world. For nine months, she was His dwelling place. And I wondered if she found her home in Him.

I cradled Dineo in my lap and pictured Jesus wrapped in swaddling clothes. How He lived and grew inside Mary for nine months, just like Dineo wriggled and twisted in my swollen abdomen before the doctor pulled her out. No longer could I protect her from the harsh realities of the world. She was safer inside. I wondered if Mary thought the same thing about her baby boy.

I marveled over the wonder of God becoming flesh and making His dwelling among us (John 1:14). How He left not only the safety of Mary's womb, but the glory of heaven for a dirty, crowded stable. How He dwelled not only *among* humankind as a baby, then man, but chooses to dwell *within* anyone who believes He is the Lord. Not only is He Emmanuel, God with us—He is God *in* us. This symbiotic mystery in which I am His dwelling place (1 Cor. 3:16), and He is mine (Deut. 33:27; Ps. 90:1). God is my home, and my body is His temple. Not just for nine months, either. His Spirit lives and grows in me from now until He comes again. An inexpressible gift—even greater than the joy of my baby girl growing inside.

CHAPTER 15

MOTHERHOOD

"He gently leads those that have young."

—Isaiah 40:11

As I grew into motherhood, a new version of home grew into me. My entire identity as a mom developed on South African turf. I felt myself drifting ever so gradually away from America as my home, as I discovered the miracle of gripe water and learned to call diapers "nappies." We shopped for a pram instead of a stroller, and debated the pros and cons of introducing a dummy, which I'd only ever known as a pacifier. Instead of liquid Tylenol, the options for children included Panado and Calpol. As Dineo developed and learned new things, so did I.

I looked into her pitch-black eyes and asked her, "Who will you become?" As I felt the pull of South Africa's cultural tide in the core of my being, I asked myself the same question. I watched Dineo change daily, and knew I couldn't escape a similar fate. No matter which books I read or which schedules I attempted to follow, I couldn't keep up. Change and routine alternated shifts until I succumbed to the inevitable reality—life would never be quite the same, and neither would I. The foundations of home shifted underfoot once again.

The early months of my pregnancy were marked by the unexpected loss of Kagiso's uncle. Death changed us. But that was not the end. My pregnancy culminated in a miraculous new life. An abundance of gifts—and I saw the gospel. I saw the effects of sin in this fallen, broken world. The pain that comes with death and loss. And I saw the promise of new life in Christ—the One who can do immeasurably more than all we ask or imagine (Eph. 3:20). I cradled my newborn and my fingertips touched the fragility of life—the realization that this home is only temporary. It's not the end—there is more to come.

Within a couple of months after Dineo's birth, we managed to raise enough money from family and friends for me to fly to the States with her. My mom was the only member of my side of the family who had met Dineo, and Sarah was beyond eager to squeeze her niece. When Sarah heard we were coming, she and her fiancé, Kent, decided to plan their wedding in three months just so I could be there for the ceremony.

In the weeks leading up to our trip, my four-month-old developed a strong case of separation anxiety. As in, she outright wailed if anyone other than me so much as looked at her the wrong way. Including Kagiso. It made for some interesting (and tiring) days, given her screams if I even attempted to place her on someone else's lap. *Oh Lord,* I prayed. *Please let her get over this before we get to America!* I couldn't bear to think of her bawling when my sister or mom tried to hold her in the limited moments they would have with her.

The time came for us to leave Cape Town, and off we went, me with a backpack secured on my shoulders, a baby strapped across my chest in a borrowed red Baby Bjorn carrier, pulling a fully loaded suitcase on wheels. The majority of people who saw us—both fellow travelers and airline personnel—had pity on me and directed me to the front of every line. Dineo was small enough to fit into the airline-provided bassinet, which hinged onto the cabin wall, but of course she refused to sleep in it. The greatest test came when I had to go to the bathroom. Sitting on an airplane toilet in cramped quarters with a wriggling baby in your lap is not for the fainthearted.

After over twenty-eight hours of travel, we finally arrived. Sarah and Kent were waiting on the couch at Mom's house well after midnight when I shuffled in, battle weary. I prayed and prayed that Dineo would let Sarah hold her. Sarah reached out to cradle her niece, and Dineo just stared into her aunt's eyes. Quiet. I breathed a long-held sigh of relief and a silent prayer of thanks to God.

Our days in Michigan were precious gifts. I proudly stood as matron of honor in Sarah and Kent's beautiful winter wedding, while my cousin walked the back halls of the building with Dineo. My adorable, world-traveling child screamed during the entire ceremony, and my poor cousin missed the whole thing.

Though I knew we had to go back to Cape Town, I didn't want to leave. If Kagiso had been with me, I would have fought to stay. South Africa had changed me; motherhood had changed me; Michigan had changed without me—yet my security blanket was still woven of the fabric of Holland. I knew how she felt against my skin. I could drop my shoulders and rest easy in her. I didn't have to think twice about the fastest way to get to the grocery store, or where to find the best deal on new shoes. My car steered itself on the same roads I'd known all my life. I could leave my mind on cruise control and sit back. In many ways, Michigan still felt like my home—and yet my daughter was just visiting. For Dineo, everything was brand-new. She didn't know my dad's dog, or the smell of my grandma's perfume. She didn't know the sound of the piano at church, or the wetness of a snowflake on her cheek. The disconnect panged me. I wanted my home to be hers. I wanted her to grow up on the shores of Lake Michigan, climbing icebergs in the winter and doing underwater handstands in July. I wanted her childhood to be shaped by the same sand I used to mold into sandcastles, the same snow I had sledded and skied down.

Instead, the Lord ripped my white knuckles from their tight grip on the comforts of home and plunked me back on another airplane. I started to notice a pattern—God always had a different plan. In my heart I mapped my own course, but the Lord established my steps (Prov. 16:9). I wrestled Him through many tears and reluctantly dumped my will onto the airplane tray when the flight attendant asked if she could take my trash. My job was to sit down on the plane; He would determine the place to land.

Dineo's first year passed, and our house-sitting gig ended. We moved again, this time to a second-floor apartment owned by our church in the heartbeat of the city. A stark contrast from the sleepy coastal suburb of the previous twelve months. We lived across the street from a grocery store called Checkers—convenient, since we shared one car. VW minibus taxis called *kombis* hooted day and night, yelling out the window for more customers to fill their seats. Car guards paced up and down the block, collecting coins as tips for watching parked vehicles. Fluorescent restaurant signs drew loud-laughing couples inside every evening.

Dineo baptized our new flat with scraps from her high chair and discarded bottles of milk. She started walking in that new apartment, and we found our feet there too. Her contagious smile attracted the affection of everyone she met—the retired Afrikaans mechanic next door, the Congolese refugees upstairs, the Rastafarian caretaker with blue overalls and long dreadlocks. She charmed the two guys who sat on the curb selling beaded crafts and the old man who worked the produce section at Checkers.

When her first birthday rolled around in July 2006, nobody from my side of the family was there to celebrate with us. The moment seared in my memory. I wanted all my people in one place. I wanted Betty Crocker boxed cake and Hudsonville ice cream. I wanted familiar.

As I walked across the parking lot of our block of flats to get something out of the car, the sharp ache of missing home stopped me short in my tracks. It welled up like a pot boiling over, sizzling onto the cold July ground as I doubled over in a near-fetal position. Black asphalt taunted me, swirling around in my tear-filled eyes. I hugged the backs of my knees while my shoulders heaved. I wept for all that I would never know. For everything my mom and Sarah would miss, and for all that Dineo would never experience as long as I kept her on the tip of Africa. I sobbed over more than missed family birthday celebrations. My mom had already missed Dineo's first words and smiles and steps. Dineo had missed a year's worth of hugs and kisses and stories that could've been read on Grandma's lap. Her first birthday broke the dam of pent up disappointment.

It's not worth it! I screamed inside. *It hurts too much. This whole overseas, cross-cultural living thing just isn't worth it!* It was my daughter's first birthday, and I was the one having a toddler-sized tantrum. I thought of my American friend who was in a new but serious relationship with a South African man, and I wanted to call her right then and tell her it wasn't worth it. The cost was too great.

CHAPTER 16

COMEBACK

"I will take refuge in the shadow of your wings until the disaster has passed."

—Psalm 57:1

Less than a year after Dineo's first birthday, I was well into my second pregnancy. In early May 2007, four weeks before I was due to give birth, the phone rang at our apartment. "Hi, honey. It's Mom." An unsettled tone in her voice betrayed her usual chipper manner.

"What's wrong?" I asked.

She hesitated. "I got a little behind in my house payments," she confessed. "Every month I thought I would catch up, but I just never quite had enough to cover it. The bank sent me a few letters and I tried to figure out a way, but . . ." Her voice trailed off. I waited. Processing. "I ran out of time." Another pause. "The bank is going to take the house." A sudden pang pierced my stomach.

"What? What do you mean, they're taking the house? Can they do that? Can't you go talk to them or something?" Mom's sobs escaped in full force. Her audible anguish dissipated my initial anger.

Still, questions swarmed in my mind: *How could this be happening? Why hadn't she told us sooner? Was she too embarrassed? Was she too proud to ask for help?*

Maybe it was all of the above, or maybe none. It didn't matter. It was too late.

The house was gone.

The first time we lost our home, I was seven years old. I lost my dad's daily presence and my house in the same season. Then the Lord gave us the renovated pump house, and gratitude only partially filled me. I felt relieved to have a place to live, but thought I deserved more. Ten rental years later, the cottage got snatched away with little warning from our landlord, after he decided to sell the property.

With Grandma's help, we got our own home. That became the house where I graduated from high school, where I returned on college breaks, where I lounged on the blue leather couch in the basement and fell asleep watching movies with my mom while she snored in the striped chair next to me. It was the house I left when I moved to South Africa, the house I brought my fiancé back to for visits, the house where we planned our American wedding ceremony. It was the house where Dineo first met her aunt, uncle, and great-grandma.

With one phone call, what once seemed so concrete and secure crumbled into a heap of debris. And all I could rescue were the memories.

I knew all things happened in the Lord's perfect timing, but from a human perspective, the house foreclosure couldn't have come at a worse time. Mom was still working at an elementary school, I was eight months pregnant with my second baby, and we both desperately wanted her to be there for the birth. Multiple phone calls crossed the Atlantic. Finally, good news: Mom's principal granted her permission to leave work a week before the school year ended so she could be in Cape Town in time for my scheduled Caesarean section. "But first," Mom added over the phone, "I have to empty the house before I leave." Relief sunk to dread. "I've started going through things. What do you want me to do with your prom dresses? And what about your artwork from high school, your yearbooks, and your scrapbooks?"

It felt surreal to realize that the last time I left the States was the last time I would ever see the inside of that house. I tried not to think about it. It ached too much to realize that a third home of ours was gone.

Home had a way of slipping away. Like the uncertainty of life when Mom had cancer, when a question mark hung over every tomorrow, I couldn't trust home to stay.

Days before my scheduled C-section, countless friends frantically helped Mom pack up her belongings, dispersing boxes and Rubbermaid totes to numerous basements and garages around town. Mom stuffed her car to the brim with last minute odds and ends, and left Sarah and Kent to clean up the aftermath as she whisked off to the airport to meet her newest grandbaby. To say it was a tense period would be an understatement. Mom left for Africa with no idea where she would live upon her return. She was homeless.

Mom landed in Cape Town on May 28, 2007. The next morning, she tagged along while Kagiso drove me to the hospital for my C-section. I showed up in the parking lot with no contractions and told the porter at the door, "I'm here to have a baby." He promptly attended to me with a wheelchair and rolled me up to the maternity ward.

By 9:05 a.m., the doctor exclaimed, "It's a boy!" We named him Caleb Aobakwe and prayed that he would follow the Lord wholeheartedly, just like the Caleb of the Bible (Num. 14:24, 32:12; Deut. 1:36; Josh. 14:14). In Setswana, Aobakwe means "the Lord be praised."

Kagiso came back that evening with Dineo. She sat still on the fake leather chair next to my bed and stared in amazement at the wonder of the new baby in her arms. She couldn't pronounce the name Caleb, so she called him "Tayib" and doted on him as a prized possession.

After three nights in the hospital, Kagiso came to take Caleb and me home. When our red Honda Ballade pulled into our apartment block, Mom and Dineo were waiting outside the building with a huge, multicolored Welcome Home poster. Dineo could hardly get inside fast enough to see her new baby brother again. Every time we had Caleb out of his crib, even if he was still fast asleep, Dineo pointed to him and announced with glee, "Tayib a-WAKE!"

That first week at home, I noticed that Mom was constantly short of breath. She mentioned it in a phone call before she came to Cape Town, but the concern got swallowed up in the packing drama, somewhere between "What should I do with your scrapbooking stuff?" and "What about your saxophone?"

"I went to see my family doctor," she told me over the phone before her visit. "He thinks my shortness of breath is probably just a recurrence of childhood asthma. He didn't seem worried. He prescribed an inhaler and told me to have a great trip."

During her time with us, the shortness of breath grew so severe that even taking a shower became strenuous. She came out of the bathroom each morning and needed to rest. In her condition, just walking across the street to the grocery store made her so winded that she had to stop for a break before entering the shop. Truncated breaths emerged—staccato quarter notes longing to be whole.

I kept trying to convince Mom to go to a physician in Cape Town, but she thought it best to wait until she could see her regular doctor. "I'll be fine," she insisted. "Besides, my doctor at home knows my whole history. It's better to wait." Despite my urging her to slow down, to sit, to rest, Mom kept plugging away. She couldn't *not* serve. It was her lifeblood. Between labored breaths, she read countless books to Dineo, changed the same number of diapers, and washed just as many dishes. She baked trays of cookies and dozens of cupcakes for the steady flow of visitors, wheezing and gasping the whole time. *It's just asthma*, I told myself over and over. *She'll be fine.*

With two kids under twenty-two months, I didn't know which way was up. Piles of clean diapers towered all over the flat and I kept grabbing the wrong size for the wrong kid. I couldn't find matching socks to save my life, never mind time to wash my hair. Meanwhile, Mom fought for a decent breath. She sat down only when necessary. I hated to see her suffer, yet I didn't know what I would've done without her during those weeks. Her presence anchored me. I knew everything would be okay, simply because she was there. Besides, Dineo adored her grandma. All was right in the world as long as Grandma was near. Even if we were just sitting on the couch, exhausted, her closeness brought comfort.

After several weeks doting on her grandchildren and helping me around the house while I recovered, the time arrived for Mom to go back to Michigan. I could hardly pry her away from my kids. Even at two years old, Dineo knew the weight of good-bye. I saw it in the quiver of her lips, and it crushed me. Some people say absence makes the heart grow fonder. I say absence just plain makes the heart hurt.

When Mom's plane landed in Grand Rapids, her breathing was so bad that she was confined to a wheelchair in the airport terminal. The next morning, she had an appointment with her doctor. That very day, they drained two liters of fluid from her lungs. *Two liters.* How is it even possible to walk around with a full Coke bottle of fluid in your chest?

I'd just finished Caleb's evening feed in the living room while Dineo sat on the floor, happily surrounded by books. The smell of our chicken curry dinner still lingered in the air. When the landline rang, I passed the baby to Kagiso so I could answer it. Elbow leaning on the kitchen counter, I held the receiver to my ear as Mom broke the news. She'd been sitting in that very spot herself just days before, wheezing as she cradled Caleb, her newest treasure.

Her voice shook. "The cancer is back. They still call it breast cancer since that's where it originated four and a half years ago, but this time it has metastasized throughout my bones." The words spilled out fast, but measured. It was as if she were reading from a script just to set all the information free. I felt the restraint in her tone as she reined in the tears. "They drained two liters of fluid from my lungs, and found malignant cells there too."

I swallowed hard. Words escaped me. The curry smell suddenly made me feel sick. By some miracle, my voice held steady until the phone clicked after the good-bye. Then I crumpled to the floor. I shook from the inside out, a leaf in a windstorm. Only one thought filled me: *This is the beginning of the end.*

Doctors could remove a tumor in the breast with a lumpectomy or a mastectomy, but they couldn't remove her bones. It felt like the vilest of attacks, a stealthy move in a brutal war. As a Christian, I've been taught not to "hate" things—but cancer is an exception. I hate it from the soles of my feet to the clenched rage pent up in my shoulders.

I later learned that on that first day, Mom's health was in such a dangerous condition that the chemo nurses quietly questioned amongst themselves whether she would even survive the first treatment. Doctors estimated that without any treatment at all, she had six months to live. With treatment, they weren't sure how long she would last. I felt as if it were my fault that she hadn't been able to see her doctor sooner. Guilt smeared over me. I couldn't get rid of it.

Mom didn't even have a place to live. Her sedan was still packed with belongings from the feverish rush to vacate her house before traveling to Cape Town. Back in the States, she crashed on the couch in my grandma's condo—a shuffling, heaving portrait of utter dependency on Christ. I couldn't imagine how low she must have felt during that time, and I was powerless to do anything but pray from a distance.

Then God bowed low, scooped her up, and gently laid her in a beautiful condo, rent-free. Owned by a friend of a friend who lived overseas, it sounded too good to be true. Mom only had to pay utilities. A gift from above, wrapped in the shape of mercy. Friends and family moved her furniture even as she sat in the oncologist's office hooked up to an IV. The hands and feet of Jesus—and me, an ocean away.

And so it began again. Chemo. Tests. Hair loss. Scans. Waiting.

Only by God's mercy did I steer clear of that former pit of despair, the one that took so long to crawl out of almost five years before, during Mom's first diagnosis. Like the time I found myself trapped beneath the raft in the rapids of the Kern River, I was flailing—and yet I had peace.

For six months, I buried myself in the immediate needs of my kids. I answered Dineo's incessant questions with as much patience as I could muster. Caleb's smiles carried me. We took frequent walks to the store, the library, the park. Anything to keep busy. Day by day, step after step, one moment of grace at a time—but my mind never wandered far from the cancer. God's grace was sufficient—but my longing was real. I desperately wanted to be with my mom. Just to sit with her. Watch TV and laugh at dumb jokes with her. Drive her to chemo treatments, each eating a Frosty from Wendy's in the freezing cold November air. I didn't care what we did—I just ached to be present.

Then one Sunday after church in November 2007, a friend drew Kagiso aside. "If you need to go, go. Don't worry about the airfare. I'll take care of it."

It was one of those moments when I tasted such lavish grace of God that I wanted to hold it on my tongue forever. All I could do was bow low in humble adoration to my Lord, who paved the runway in such an unexpected, mysterious way.

We accepted the offer, never quite getting up from our knees. Before we flew to the States for Thanksgiving and Christmas, I tried to thank the generous benefactor. In lieu of words, my gratitude poured out in welled up tears. I swiped the back of my hand across my face in embarrassment—but the salty residue of thankfulness left an indelible mark.

When our fourth and final flight landed after more than thirty hours of travel, I walked down the last arrivals corridor, shoulder muscles screaming for rest. My gray

New Balance shoes hugged more snugly than usual. My throbbing feet had frequented the same stretch of carpet numerous times—but that time was different. On every other trip, without fail, come rain, storm, or hail, the same smiling eyes that soothed me to sleep as an infant were waiting to greet me at the end of the corridor.

I wrestled my brain into concession, forcing it to accept the present reality: *She's too sick to come to the airport.*

We arrived at her condo. The same thought seemed to be in all of our minds: "This is the last Christmas you'll spend together. Make the most of it." Mom was so convinced she would never see another Christmas this side of heaven that she gave away some of her favorite Christmas ornaments to her closest friends.

We savored the moments, the traditions, the memories—cutting down our own Christmas tree, bumping along on the horse-drawn wagon ride at the tree farm, sipping hot cider in the frigid air. Mom held and hugged her grandchildren as often as possible, pressing her love into them as if she hoped they would still feel her embrace long after she was gone. We attended the traditional Christmas Eve service at my home church and sang "Silent Night" in the dark, handheld candles our only source of light. We belly-laughed when two-year-old Dineo emerged from the bedroom wearing a new Christmas dress and, with a twirl, quoted from the movie *Cinderella*, "It's a wonderful dream come true!" And yet the tension remained—a knot in my stomach hindering my appetite for abandoned joy.

Grief came to visit often. He occupied the empty chair at the table and made his presence known whenever the conversation lulled. Sometimes he stayed for the weekend. We saw his reflection in the eyes of people at church on Sunday mornings. Then the visits grew even longer, until eventually he just decided to move in for good. And by then, I couldn't kick him out—he was part of the family.

After a blessed and full six weeks, during the first week of January 2008, our time in the States drew to a close. It was one of the hardest good-byes. Everyone I loved most was with me in the same place. On previous trips, I had family on both sides of the ocean. Did we really have to go back? Tears flowed as they always did. I swiped them away, wishing I could do the same to the sick feeling in my stomach. After multiple hugs, the Lord pried me out of my mom's embrace. And I turned my back, not knowing if I'd ever see her again.

Over time, I got used to the permanent companion of grief. Whenever someone asked with genuine concern, "How's your mom doing?" I learned to camouflage the hurt, always taking the shape of a pasted-on smile. Some weeks, I just didn't know what to say. She'd rally, then worsen, and I grew tired of forcing my lips into that plastic smile. But I did what I had to do. I fed my kids multiple times a day, wiped their noses, tied their shoes. I made the beds, swept the floor, scrubbed the tub. I peeled my heart from my sleeve, slipped it into my pocket, and waited for the stolen moments of solitude when I could weep unnoticed.

Every day was a battle. Hand-to-hand combat. The ache increased with each test result, until eventually even the victories tasted like defeat. My senses were numbed by the constant fatigue of the fight and the nagging conviction that the war was already lost. Occasionally, Mom, Sarah, and I found temporary relief from our posts in the trenches—maybe a good test result or a diminished side effect—but we knew it wasn't for long. Soon we would rotate duty back to the front line, where the stench of death permeated the air.

Hope slipped through my fingers like the slow, steady seeping of water through cupped hands. And I let it fall.

One Sunday back in Cape Town, a gracious doctor friend from church asked me how my mom was doing. Instead of the generic, "Okay," or "She's hanging in there," I gave him an honest answer, assuming that with his profession, he could handle the truth. "She's not doing so well," I confessed, standing in the back of our sanctuary after the morning service. It felt refreshing to speak the truth, and yet the admission seemed like a betrayal against the lies I'd been telling myself.

In all gentleness, with his kind eyes and white-haired wisdom, he said to me, "You know something? In the grand scheme of things, we all have a terminal illness. Since birth, we've all been under palliative care." His response could have come across as discouraging. Maybe even offensive. Instead, it was exactly what I needed to hear. Sometimes it just takes the right words at the right moment from the right friend to shift perspective and help the light come into view. I needed that shift to help me see that things could've been much worse. Mom could've been hell-bound. She could've died instantly without warning. Not that her circumstances lessened the grief or the pain—but her position in Christ gave great comfort. A green shoot of hope springing forth from dark, stubborn soil.

I used to think this life was about healing. Eventually, I learned it's about dying—dying to self, dying to sin, dying to the world . . . so that in the next life, I can be made whole. So I die a little every day, until true living becomes the art of dying well.

CHAPTER 17

ADOPTED

"In love he predestined us for adoption to himself as sons through Jesus Christ, according to the purpose of his will, to the praise of his glorious grace."

—Ephesians 1:4–6 ESV

Over the next year, Mom's health teetered. She would find a strain of chemotherapy that seemed to work for a while, and then it was as if the cancer figured out what was happening and abruptly resisted the drug. The tumor marker count would climb, and Mom's oncologist would come up with another option. I continued to push the nagging question aside: *How long until we run out of options?*

Back in Cape Town, life continued. A year after our six-week trip to Michigan, Dineo was nearly three-and-a-half, and Caleb was toddling around, a sturdy and determined eighteen-month-old. Friends pooled together and once again provided plane tickets for Dineo and me to visit my mom for Thanksgiving.

Then on Wednesday, November 19, 2008, we woke up to learn that Kagiso's six-year-old cousin, Kabelo, had lost his mom. Kabelo's dad was Kagiso's uncle who died four years earlier, when I was pregnant with Dineo. Overnight, Kabelo became one of the three million orphans of South Africa.

Months earlier, I had read a statistic that South Africa had more HIV-infected people than any other country in the world. The scourge of AIDS left tremendous needs in its wake. Kagiso and I shared the same burden that something must be done. "We could adopt a child we don't know," Kagiso reasoned aloud one day in the car. "Or we could look to the needs within our own family. The second option seems to make more sense to me." When Kagiso's uncle died, Kagiso and I prayed regularly about the possibility of adopting Kabelo, but never mentioned our prayers or desires to anyone else.

Kabelo had been living with Kagiso's aunt in Pretoria that year to receive better care. Together they took the four-hour bus ride to Kimberley for Kabelo's mom's funeral. That Wednesday morning after the funeral, we also learned that changing family dynamics meant that Kabelo was no longer able to stay in Pretoria and needed a place to live. Kagiso and I looked at each other upon hearing the news. Our eyes conveyed the same conviction: "He needs to come here."

After a flurry of phone calls over two days, Kagiso and his mom were on the road to Kimberley to bring Kabelo home. I took Dineo and Caleb to my mother-in-law's house to stay with Kagiso's brother and cousin, who lived with her. I had no idea how our lives were about to change, and yet I was confident that it was the right thing to do.

Whether I was ready or not, we were about to become a family of five.

After the nine-hour car ride to Cape Town, Kabelo arrived late Saturday night with one black suitcase, a wide smile, and pockets full of Pokémon cards. No toothbrush. He called me "mom" right away, and proved to be a very loving, loud boy, craving attention and affection.

The next morning, Kagiso left early to prepare for church, while I remained to shepherd a boy who spoke no English. I pieced together sentences out of fragmented Afrikaans, Setswana, and English phrases, aided by lots of flamboyant hand motions. By no small miracle, I managed to get all three kids fed, dressed, and out the door in time for the ten o'clock church service. At church, Kabelo zipped from one person to the next—inside the building, outside, then in again, smiling and speaking Afrikaans the whole time. He wore me out as I tried in vain to keep track of his whereabouts. He certainly didn't fit the stereotype of one fresh out of trauma.

The next morning Dineo and I waved good-bye to Kagiso, Kabelo, and Caleb, and boarded a plane bound for the States. From a human perspective, the timing was less than ideal. I feared Kabelo wouldn't understand—first he watched his biological mom's body get lowered into the ground, and then this new woman who he called "mom" disappeared down an airport terminal. I kept reassuring him as best I could with English and hand motions, "I'll be back. I'm coming back." Yet God used those two weeks for Kagiso to forge a bond with Kabelo, to teach him house rules and get him acclimated to his new environment. Plus, Kagiso spoke both Afrikaans and Setswana—the two languages Kabelo understood.

The spontaneous generosity from South African peers that made our ten-day trip possible not only gave me an immense sense of gratitude, it also taught me what it means to be the church. To live as one body, to carry each other's burdens. I saw how God's provision spans across cultures and expectations. I also saw the importance of serving with the resources and means we've been given. Some people open their pockets to sponsor a reunion for a cancer-filled woman and her daughter and granddaughter; others open their door to a parentless child.

Because the time span in which we decided to adopt and the day we welcomed Kabelo into our home was so short, various friends questioned our decision. Most were supportive, but some were taken aback by the abrupt change. Raised eyebrows revealed their uncertainty about whether we knew what we were doing. Truthfully, we had no idea. We were just trying to obey.

While Kagiso reined in the boys in Cape Town, I spent Thanksgiving in Michigan with a talkative three-year-old who told everyone she met about her new brother. Dineo built miniature snowmen on Grandma's kitchen counter while I flipped open my computer and showed visiting friends photos of our new family of five—four of us smiling, and Caleb looking skeptical. Perhaps rightfully so.

After Dineo and I enjoyed our jaunt to Michigan and settled back into our apartment in Cape Town, Kagiso returned to work and left me at home with three kids.

I'd grown into motherhood with my one- and three-year-old, but the abrupt addition of a six-year-old bundle of energy jarred me. My childhood consisted of a houseful of females. The extent of my knowledge raising boys capped at eighteen months. Although Dineo talked my ear off, she wasn't overly rambunctious. She was often content to color next to me or "read" books to her dolls. Suddenly I had a loud, active boy on my hands, and I didn't know where to start. The things he found funny weren't funny to me. He wasn't content to sit on the floor doing puzzles or looking at books. Like many kids that age, he wanted to run, climb, and jump.

I grew a lot through our adoption process. Because both of Kabelo's parents were deceased, the legal aspect was simple—we didn't have to wait to get written permission for custody. He was already living with us, so we never experienced the agonizing wait that many adoptive parents endure before they can hold their children in their arms. But in countless other ways, God used the experience to refine me. He daily made me aware of my shortcomings and my desperate need for Him.

During those early weeks and months, God taught me faith. Kagiso and I had no way of knowing how things would turn out. We clung to the conviction that this was where the Lord was leading and walked forward into the darkness, unable to see what might lay ahead in the path. It was scary and exhausting. I stubbed my toes on unseen rocks and tripped over fallen logs. The language barrier bruised me. I learned more Afrikaans in our first two weeks together than I'd learned in six years.

The need for constant behavioral correction chafed—I felt as if I was always saying no. The apartment that I childproofed for a one- and three-year-old didn't deter a six-year-old from climbing onto countertops and reaching a box of matches in the kitchen cupboard while I was in the shower. I came out of the bathroom and smelled the residue of smoke in the air. When I realized what had happened, I was furious. I yelled. I barely managed to keep my true feelings in my head, but it didn't matter. God knew what was in my heart: *I didn't bring you into this house just so you could burn it down with my other two kids inside!*

Every morning, I prayed for more patience. And though I failed daily, God never stopped giving grace.

CHAPTER 18

VISIT

"Grandchildren are the crown of the aged."

—Proverbs 17:6 ESV

When Kagiso and I got married, we made an agreement. If the Lord willed, after our children were born, we would spend the first five years of their lives in South Africa and the second five years in the States before returning to South Africa. We wanted our kids to experience America at an age when they would remember it. We hoped they would forge real-life relationships with my side of the family and get to experience American culture for themselves.

A few months after Kabelo joined our family, we began to make plans for the big move overseas. Mom was not doing well, and it seemed a good time to go. Then, in the process of obtaining Kabelo's birth certificate and applying for his passport, we learned about an international governmental agreement called the

Hague Inter-country Adoption Convention. Because of stipulations in this agreement, and because I was an American adopting a South African child, I was required to reside with Kabelo in South Africa for two full years after the adoption was finalized. We would have to wait twenty-three more months before we would be free to move.

My heart split wide open. I felt trapped in a foreign country. I prayed right there, staring blankly at the filthy tile blocks on the government office floor. A desperate plea to my God: *Lord, if my mom or my dad dies within this two-year waiting period, please don't allow me to be bitter toward you or anyone else.* I knew the frailty of my spirit, the deceptiveness of my heart. The way I would want to blame someone, even God. I begged God to help me to be strong in the face of this unexpected blow.

In April 2009, five months after Kabelo arrived, Mom entered a season of oral chemo. Instead of going in to the oncology office every week to sit in a chair and have the chemotherapy given to her intravenously, she took chemotherapy pills every morning at home. Mom saw the transition as a window of opportunity—since our plans to move to the U.S. had been postponed, she determined to visit Cape Town to meet her newest grandson. She had met Kabelo briefly at our wedding five years earlier, but had no idea at that time that one day he would be her grandchild.

We deliberated, weighing the pros and cons of Mom making the trip. Her oncologist granted her permission to travel, but there were risks. The cancer might unexpectedly become more aggressive while she was away. The oral chemo might stop working. The fluid in her lungs might increase. She could have difficulty breathing on the plane. Any number of dangers could emerge.

Mom, Sarah, and I agonized over the decision. I wanted what was best for Mom, but I didn't know what that was. I knew it would be physically taxing for her to visit, but couldn't bear to deny her the joy of seeing her grandkids. I didn't see how I could say no to her coming and not feel horrible about it—but I also knew I'd never forgive myself if she came and the trip proved detrimental to her health. Emails and phone calls fired back and forth as we discussed the pros and cons.

We sought advice from several friends. The consensus was to consider the potential health hazards but to leave the decision to Mom. One of my friends worked extensively with terminally ill patients. She pointed out, "Your mom is the only one who knows what it's like to live in her shoes. Many patients I've seen often have an internal debate about quality of life versus quantity of life. They ask themselves, 'Do I want to live longer and not enjoy it, or should I take a potential risk and do something meaningful?' Most of them end up taking risks for the sake of doing something they love."

I even emailed one of Mom's surgeons, a Christian man named Dr. DeCook. I asked whether he thought Mom should make the trip. He responded with these words:

I think your mom's health is somewhat miraculous. Living and breathing every day is somewhat miraculous for all of us, but especially so for your mom. For all of her oncologist's careful ministrations, we are not really sure why she is still doing so well. I don't think there is anything about being in South Africa that would necessarily put her out of that somewhat tenuous, but also miraculous, position she is in.

Having talked to your mom about you and those grandchildren, I can hear the anguish in her voice to see them, be with them, be part of their living and breathing memories. I don't think Skype can quite compensate for that.

If something happened to your mom's health here in the US, you both would feel TERRIBLE if she hadn't taken this opportunity to be together. And there is certainly no guarantee that nothing would happen in the US.

Honestly, if I was your mother, I would move to South Africa semi-permanently. I don't think the Judsons or the Careys or the Studds or the Livingstones or the Schweitzers or any of those early missionaries had any idea that they would survive more than two months where they were. It was all a faith-based venture. They knew they were in God's hands. That's still true today—we just add a few layers of science and control to that truth, and sometimes forget the reality of it.

So I could, somewhat recklessly, recommend she go. But then, isn't all Real Living somewhat reckless?

Dr. D

Dr. DeCook was right. All real living is reckless. All living requires faith. All life is miraculous. In the end, Mom booked tickets to arrive in June and stay for two months.

On June 19, my fifth wedding anniversary, I sent this email to friends:

Mom is scheduled to fly to Cape Town for a visit next week. The tentative plan is for her to come for two months.

Since booking the ticket, a scan has revealed that the current oral chemotherapy treatment is no longer effective, and the cancerous spots in her bones (particularly shoulder, spine, and hips) are more active than they were in February. The doctor plans to change her treatment to a weekly intravenous chemo as soon as she returns to Michigan.

Some of you are aware that yesterday she had to have fluid drained from her right lung again. The doctor said that if the lung should collapse during the procedure, she would not be allowed to fly. Mom prayed and asked the Lord to give her a sign—if He did not want her to travel, she asked that He would allow her lung to collapse. It did not. They managed to successfully drain 650 ml of fluid with no puncture. However, she is not feeling so great after the procedure, and will have to wait to see if she recovers enough to fly the 28 hours it will take to get here.

Mom did regain enough strength to board the airplane the following week. Looking back, it was a rash decision. But that's what love looks like. Love is rash and blind and often desperate. Love does crazy things.

Mom survived the transatlantic travel with the backing of countless prayers. Her face was radiant. I never saw her as happy as when she had all three grandchildren wrapped around her shoulders. It's strange how time feels more valuable when you're aware that you don't have much of it. We savored each moment and etched memories into cameras and grateful hearts.

Mom colored many pictures and read even more books aloud—just like when I was a kid. She took each of her grandchildren out on a special one-on-one date, treating Dineo to an ice-cream sundae bigger than her head. We played in the sand at Camp's Bay and revisited the Sinfull ice-cream parlor, seven years after Mom's first taste on the night of my twenty-first birthday.

We frequented parks on the sunny afternoons, and spent the chilly evenings curled up under blankets on the couch watching Little Einstein DVDs. Friends from church treated Mom and me to an afternoon in the winelands. We drank in the most magnificent views and didn't want to wake up from the dream.

Mom baked cupcakes and cakes with plenty of eager helping hands. We celebrated Dineo's fourth birthday and my twenty-eighth. We grilled at Kagiso's mom's house and made s'mores in the fireplace. We set up picnics and Play-Doh on our balcony and played make-believe. If only we could've pretended a world without cancer.

We even took the cable car up Table Mountain with the kids and Kagiso's mom. Dineo had been to the top when she was a year old, but the boys had never been. As we waited in line, we watched one gondola-like contraption ascend the mountain, while the other carried passengers down from the peak.

When our turn to board finally came, we clambered in with much excitement. The kids raced for a position near the windows, necks craned to get a good view. Mom joined them at first, smiling and laughing at their enthusiasm. Before the cable car left the boarding station, the attendant made an announcement:

"Please be aware that the floor of the cable car rotates everywhere except in this middle section where I'm standing. If anyone does not wish to stand on moving floor, make your way to this middle pole."

Mom's eyes grew big. Without hesitation, she reached out and grabbed the pole. As the cable car left the station, I glanced over at Mom. She clamped her eyes shut, face drained of color. The rest of us circled slowly around her, though our feet remained planted. We got a 360-degree view of our surroundings—it was breathtaking.

While others *oohed* and *aahed*, Mom gritted her teeth and prayed for the cable car to hurry up. Once we reached the summit, we exited the car and were greeted by the most amazing views. It was glorious. To one side, the Atlantic stretched indefinitely. To the other, the Twelve Apostles stood as majestic sentries guarding Table Mountain's back. The city bowl bustled silently below, trees, cars, and buildings dotting the sweeping landscape.

There's no way to see this view except from the top of the mountain. It can only be appreciated one way—from the peak.

Mom's cancer was like that cable car ride. While the rest of the world stood on the fringes and slowly circled by, Mom closed her eyes and held on tight to the center pole. She knew good things awaited her at the top of the mountain, she just didn't like having to get there. But she hunkered down without complaint, gripped the unmoving anchor of Christ, and let Him carry her to the top.

Mom's two months in Cape Town passed quickly. Her health held up better than expected, but toward the end of her visit, her shortness of breath increased—not as bad as the time she visited for Caleb's birth, but still noticeable. Way too soon, it was time for another round of good-byes. They never got easier. As with every other separation, my stomach knotted for days before her imminent departure. Once more, I didn't know if I would see her again this side of heaven.

Two weeks after landing back in the States, Mom wrote this on her blog:

> *My time in South Africa was truly a gift from God, and I am so thankful I made the decision to go. The children kept me laughing all day long, and we were able to do so many things outside because of the unusual, beautiful weather! We played at the beach many times and went to several parks, the Waterfront to see the seals in the water and watch the boats, took a trip via cable car up to Table*

Mountain on a very mild day, and just all the play that happens throughout the day.

I read tons of books to the kids each day, my favorite thing to do, played with clay, painted, and a very special time was bedtime. We read the Bible, prayed, and I sang to them when the lights went out. I will always remember the wonderful days I had with my family. I did miss Sarah and Kent, my mom, and friends, too, but Kate and Kagiso's friends were the essence of hospitality . . . amazing times with so many . . . being invited for meals or tea, given gifts and prayers. The church had me come up front the last Sunday I was there before going home and they prayed for me. It is a very special community of believers!

Two weeks later, she was admitted to the hospital. Once again, I was helpless in South Africa, relying on updates from my sister. Mom's shortness of breath stemmed from the cancerous fluid building up in the lining of her lungs. Nurses drained fluid from both sides, but had to stop prematurely because the procedure caused Mom too much pain.

An echocardiogram revealed additional fluid around Mom's pericardium, the lining around her heart. A cardiologist tried unsuccessfully to drain the fluid, did a blood transfusion because of low hemoglobin levels, and scheduled Mom for surgery. The doctor planned to make a "window" in the pericardium to allow the fluid to drain naturally from Mom's heart to her lungs. He would then put in two semi-permanent drains, one from each lung. This would allow her to drain the fluid herself from home, rather than having to go back to the hospital each week.

Again, Sarah shouldered the burden of caring for Mom. I wanted to be there more than anything else. I was grateful for the temporary distraction of my kids during the day, but nights were hard. I tried to sleep, but worry kept me awake. In those lonely moments, fear rushed in and wreaked quiet havoc. Tears came often, slipping silently onto my pillow. I didn't want Kagiso to know I was crying. Again. He had enough to deal with and couldn't do anything to help me, anyway.

Over time, I even developed chest pains and an accelerated heart rate. I massaged the knots of tension and tried to rub the uncertainty out of my chest, but fear of the future was locked deep beneath the skin. I called my dad, a retired non-invasive cardiologist, and explained my symptoms. With two words, he pronounced a diagnosis: "Sympathy pains."

"*What?*" I asked, incredulous.

"Sympathy pains," he repeated. "Stress. Your body is reacting to your circumstances."

Could the body really do that? I considered requesting medication from my family doctor, just to help me cope. I knew the stress was temporary and circumstantial, but it nearly overcame me.

Mom's surgery was successful, and after a total of twelve days in the hospital, she got to go home. Another hurdle scaled by the grace of God. Gradually, my chest pains subsided as well—but stress continued to dance without ceasing, just under my skin.

CHAPTER 19

IDENTITY

"A stranger and a pilgrim, I have no earthly store."

—Frederick Whitfield, "I Need Thee, Precious Jesus"

Soon after learning that we would be in South Africa longer than expected, we decided to look for a bigger place to live with a patch of grass. Our second-floor apartment with no yard was not sufficient for three busy kids. Kabelo literally shimmied up the door frames and swung from the top by curled fingertips, teaching Dineo to do the same. The once comfortable space of our three-bedroom flat compacted. We searched and searched, but couldn't find anything in a relatively safe area within our limited price range.

What we didn't realize was that life is supposed to feel tight. This earthly skin of ours is meant to get stretch marks, if we're pregnant with the hope of glory. We *should* wriggle with discomfort like our seams are about to burst, until our labor in this life is over and our hope has been delivered. With all of creation, we "groan inwardly as we wait eagerly for our adoption as sons, the redemption of our bodies" (Rom. 8:23) and we continue to "groan, longing to be clothed with our heavenly dwelling" (2 Cor. 5:2).

Through our adoption journey, even despite the setbacks, my appreciation for God's generosity grew. I saw afresh the way He stretched out His arms on the cross to welcome me, His adopted one, as His own. He didn't just clean up a spare bedroom in the basement for me to squat in for a while, nor did He build an addition onto an existing structure to make space for me. He gave me himself as my home.

Passages like Deuteronomy 33:27 took me by surprise: "The eternal God is your dwelling place" (ESV). Is that even possible? How could the psalmist write, "Lord, you have been our dwelling place" (Ps. 90:1 ESV)? Will I ever be able to wrap my mind around this concept? God himself *is my home*. Right now.

If I'm in Him and He's in me, I'm home. No matter where I live. On the other hand, as a believer in Christ, the Holy Spirit has taken up residence in my heart, and I become the dwelling place of God. It doesn't mean that this is heaven on earth—but it's a foretaste. This life is a shadow of what lies ahead, a dim and blurred reflection of what is to come. "Now we see but a poor reflection as in a mirror; then we shall see face to face. Now I know in part; then I shall know fully, even as I am fully known" (1 Cor. 13:12).

These truths helped me as we continued our search for a place to live with outdoor space. Months passed. The walls continued to close in on us. Although I knew things would get better if the kids could play outside, I also felt sad when I thought about leaving the flat. We'd been there for four years—longer than any other place I'd lived in South Africa—and it held a special place in my heart. Dineo had learned to walk on that carpet. We carried Caleb home from the hospital through that front door. Kabelo joined our family in that place. Church friends visited us there for Bible study, counseling, or just for tea—sharing, laughing, crying. We loved our neighbors, the car guards outside, the caretaker with the bright blue overalls and the long dreadlocks that dangled from his baggy cap. We loved the library up the road, and the two guys who sold their handcrafted beaded work from the curb on the corner. The kind cashiers at the grocery store across the street who always commented on Dineo's afro. The memories held in that place surpassed measuring.

Toward the end of the waiting game to get into a larger home, the 2010 FIFA World Cup was held in South Africa. For months leading up to the event, the hype escalated. A brand-new stadium was built in Green Point for the occasion. Advertisements popped up everywhere. Airfare skyrocketed. Some people even moved out of their houses temporarily to rent their space to the influx of tourists. I'd never been a die-hard soccer fan, so I didn't understand all the fuss.

Then came the opening ceremony.

Our flat was in the hub of the city's central district, and life got *loud*. People blew on plastic *vuvuzelas* day and night, up and down the streets, hanging their heads out of minibus taxis. More vehicles were decked out with flags than not—most proudly supporting South Africa, but many sporting flags from other countries.

In no time, I caught the bug. I couldn't avoid the vibe surging in the city. I became a crazy person. We even borrowed a television just so I could watch the games. I drew up a handmade bracket and taped it to the kitchen door, filling in team names, winners, and scores every time there was a match. My veins pumped patriotic pride.

Then came the moment of identity crisis—if the U.S. played South Africa, who would I support? By then, I'd lived in Cape Town for eight years. I thought about how I could finally stand in the grocery store and no longer labor to do conversions in my head, South African rand to U.S. dollars, or milliliters to cups or ounces. I could just look at the price tag and know whether it was a good deal or not. More than that, I knew what brands I trusted and wanted to buy.

Nobody warned me that it would take years of living in a foreign country before I finally felt like I sort of knew what I was doing. I even started to realize that my memory was jumbling up my country categories, as if my brain had compartments for "American things" and "South African things." After living in Cape Town for so long, I started to forget whether I'd known about certain items and brands before moving to Africa. Did I know about Colgate before Cape Town? *Yes.* Did I know about Opel cars? *I couldn't remember.* It was somewhat disconcerting, this melding of memories. The lines of home had blurred, and I couldn't tell which walls belonged to which house.

After some deliberation, the scales of my heart tipped in favor of South Africa's national soccer team, Bafana Bafana. There's nothing like two months of nonstop blowing *vuvuzelas* to solidify a girl's identity in a place. My love for South Africa was sealed. I may not be one of hers by birth, but she adopted me as her own.

Amid the World Cup frenzy, we finally found a reasonably priced rental house with an enclosed backyard. During that same period, some American missionary friends in Cape Town, the Johnsons, asked if we would look after their house and two dogs for a year while they went on furlough, starting in November that same year. We knew we wanted the house-sitting stint, but debated whether it was worth moving twice just to have a yard for four extra months. A good friend of mine with three kids reasoned, "That's one hundred and twenty days that your kids will be able to play outside! It is *so* worth it!"

We took the plunge and moved just after the World Cup ended in July. My friend was right—it was so worth it. The kids were outside more often than not. They came up with every imaginable game to play together and barely wanted to come inside when I called them for lunch.

Less than a month after we moved in, we received more surprising and scary news: my dad had to have unexpected heart bypass surgery. Sarah articulated my emotions in a blog post she wrote at the time:

> *The other day I went to work, took my mom grocery shopping (because she just can't do it by herself anymore), and called my dad to see what time I should come over the next day to mow his lawn and help with yard work.*
>
> *We found out two weeks ago that my dad would have to have triple-bypass surgery. Sooner rather than later, obviously. He's scheduled for surgery August 25 and has to take it easy until then. So I've been helping out with a few of the more strenuous items on his to-do list.*
>
> *Today, I realized his heart might not make it to surgery, or through surgery, or much longer after that. Funny. After all the time I spend coping with my mother's terminal illness, I somehow neglected to realize that my father is getting old, that death can come for him just as easily as for my mother, or for me.*

I had the same thoughts. I was so wrapped up in the uncertainty of our mom's health that I hadn't given much thought about how swiftly any of us could be taken away. In many ways, I was stressing for no reason about my mom. She had Jesus. Eternally speaking, she was fine. Even in death, she would be safe from harm. Other friends and relatives, however, didn't possess such security. They were in far graver danger if they hadn't bent a knee to the King of Kings.

When I spoke to Dad on the phone prior to his surgery, he said, "The biggest annoyance is that they have to break my sternum to get to my heart. That's what will take the longest to heal afterward." His heart condition, though potentially life-threatening, was not giving him any physical pain, per se. Yet to get to the heart, doctors had to inflict pain on him before complete healing could take place. I shuddered at the thought—but it made so much sense. How often in life do we have to endure a painful experience to be made whole? For "no discipline seems pleasant at the time, but painful. Later on, however, it produces a harvest of righteousness and peace for those who have been trained by it" (Heb. 12:11). Pain has a purpose. "Not only so, but we also rejoice in our sufferings, because we know that suffering produces perseverance; perseverance, character; and character, hope" (Rom. 5:3–4).

Surgery day arrived. The agony of distance panged once again as I awaited reports from Sarah and Angela about Dad's lengthy and risky heart procedure. Time lagged. I watched the clock, making mental conversions to account for the time difference. At last, my phone rang. Dad was awake, and the surgery had gone well. I was finally able to exhale my pent-up anxiety and fall into a deep sleep.

CHAPTER 20

GRACE

"Now to him who is able to do immeasurably more than all we ask or imagine . . ."

—Ephesians 3:20

The wind blew warm in Cape Town that afternoon. It was mid-October 2010, and life clipped along at its usual, steady beat. The proverbial foot had been lifted from the accelerator long enough to take a Sabbath rest, and we had just returned home from church. Kagiso called me to the rust-colored, fake leather couch and told me to sit down.

He handed me an unmarked envelope. I paused, perplexed. It wasn't our anniversary. It wasn't my birthday. I looked at his face for a clue, but found a blank slate. Slowly opening the mystery envelope, I pulled out an itinerary. A round-trip plane ticket. For me. From Cape Town to Michigan. Departing less than two weeks from that shocking moment. My mouth fell slack as I read and reread the sheet of paper in my trembling hand, trying desperately to process what seemed an impossibility.

The anonymous gift would allow me to be home with my mom for her fifty-ninth birthday. I was speechless. Though I had been blessed with a handful of trips home during my stay in Cape Town, none of those visits had ever fallen over her birthday. We hadn't celebrated together in person for eight years. But that year we would.

"Are you serious?!" I exclaimed, still unbelieving.

Kagiso nodded, smiling at my joy. "Yep." I hugged him, my arms still shaking, mind reeling.

"Does Mom know? Who will watch the kids?" Logistics crowded my excitement.

"Your mom doesn't know yet. I thought you'd want to tell her yourself. My mom will watch the kids. Don't worry about it; everything's figured out. You just go and enjoy the time together."

If somebody asked me to define grace, I would tell them that story. The story of God's radical favor, completely and utterly undeserved. The story of His shocking generosity, sealed in a pure white envelope and held out to all who would open a palm to receive. The story of His unexpected gift of redemption for no particular reason other than grace.

I took the surprise trip home with its perfect, unobtrusive bow, and clutched it with grateful arms and a full and heavy heart. I confessed to a friend that I was nervous about what I would find on the other side. There would be no glossy cushion of a computer screen to soften the blow. I was scared to see how bad my mom's health had gotten. How much the cancer had gnawed away. But my friend said simply, "Just enjoy it." So I packed those three words into my suitcase, and I did. I pushed back the temptation to overanalyze the challenges, for "our light and momentary troubles are achieving for us an eternal glory that far outweighs them all" (2 Cor. 4:17).

Her condo smelled like chocolate chip cookies and scented candles and death.

For the first time, I saw the massive oxygen machine in person, the one I had only heard before over Skype, with its rhythmic *bzzzt-pptsshhh . . . bzzzt-pptsshhh* boosting air into Mom's nostrils and lungs.

The clear tube that ran from the tank to her nose was miles long so she could move as freely as one can when strapped to a machine. I swear I tripped over that thing every five minutes. My foot caught on the cord and I gasped in panic, searching her face to find the tube in place, swaggered from ear to ear. It happened so often that we had to laugh about it—what else could we do?

We laughed a lot, actually. Like when she leaned in too closely to the gas oven while removing the world's best chocolate chip cookies, and smelled something other than cookies burning. A plastic smell. Leaning back, she found the fringe of her wig singed from the heat. And so we laughed some more. Then we doubled over again in the Hobby Lobby parking lot, when the wind blew so fierce that Mom instinctively held onto that same wig for fear it would blow clean away. But as the wise Solomon wrote in Proverbs, "even in laughter the heart may ache, and joy may end in grief" (14:13).

I watched her shuffle along the carpet of her condo, feet numb from neuropathy. Her slippers whispered gentle swishes and I knew that yes, "outwardly we are wasting away, yet inwardly we are being renewed day by day" (2 Cor. 4:16). Even as her body dwindled, Mom's faith stood resolute. A bulging bodyguard, shoulders back and arms crossed at the door of her soul. Nothing could separate her from the love of her God (Rom. 8:38–39).

The cocktail of drugs Mom ingested caused her to sleep late each morning, but my body was still six time zones ahead. I woke early every day, keenly aware of the oxygen tank's persistent whine. Like the rhythmic creaking of a playground swing, I knew she was still there just by the sound. I climbed out of bed and peeked into Mom's room to make sure her chest was rising and falling with the supplemental bursts of air. Relieved, I tiptoed back to my room to change into workout clothes, and then snuck outside as soundlessly as possible.

A man-made pond sprawled behind Mom's condominium. Every morning, I walked the concrete path that hugged its perimeter. Inhaling the crisp, autumn air, I could taste the vitality on my tongue, and it tasted unfair. Why should I be so healthy and full of life, when Mom lay in bed, wasting away? I held the feeling of being alive like a lozenge and it soothed my throat, sore from screaming about how much life hurt. Then the sensation dissolved, leaving the flavor of gratitude lingering behind. After watching Mom struggle to shuffle along, it felt so good to walk. Until those mornings circling the pond, I hadn't thought much about the blessing of being able to walk. As the sun rose in the autumn sky, thankfulness rose in my heart and bolstered my step. I could walk without pain, and I never wanted to take it for granted again.

God used that quiet time alone with Him to remind me that "he himself gives everyone life and breath and everything else" (Acts 17:25, NIV 2011). And so every step and every breath became a gift, and gradually, the awareness that it's all a gift. It's all a gift, and it's all pointing to *the* gift—the gift that surpasses the joy found in flying home to be with my ailing mom for a week. The gift of eventually flying home to be with my Almighty Father forever.

When the day of her birthday arrived, I showered Mom with cards and small gifts of love from friends she had made in Cape Town. The beloved church family half a world away, who held up our arms as we grew weak in battle. Mom sat on the edge of her overstuffed ivory couch wearing her wig, a huge smile, and a brace on her left arm—evidence of the brittleness of her cancer-infused bones. With numb fingers and a fractured wrist, she opened the tokens of adoration wrapped in prayer. Fragrant lotions and Rooibos tea. Devotional books and beaded jewelry.

Mom, Sarah, and I continued the celebration by driving to Grand Haven, a neighboring Lake Michigan coastal town. Huddled around a table at a ceramic painting studio, we painted, talked, and laughed. Without my husband or kids with me on that trip, it felt like I was back in high school. Just the three of us again.

"Remember the time Kate threw up in the hallway in the middle of the night, and Mom ran out of her room to help, and fell in it?"

"Remember when Mom drove away from the bank with the teller's deposit canister and tried to make us return it for her?"

Laughter and art around the same table was the perfect blend of therapy. I almost forgot the real reason I was there. Almost.

Sarah painted an oval-shaped platter, I picked a vase, and Mom chose a square plate. Mom brushed a plum color around the outer border, filled the center of the square with a teal background, and added words from Psalm 46:10 in matching plum across the plate: "Be still and know that I am God."

That was my mom.

As our brushes swiped color over the dull plaster, Sarah and I stole glances at our watches and each other. Mom had no way of knowing, but a surprise party waited at her condo. We went out for a nice dinner at one of Mom's favorite restaurants on the harbor, and then planned to head home to celebrate with friends and dessert—except she didn't know about the friends part. The clock ticked. Sarah and I didn't want to rush such a pleasant evening, but we also knew a crowd of women were sitting quietly in a dark room waiting to shout, "Surprise!"

Eventually we finished our meal and made our way step by painfully slow step from the restaurant to the parking lot. Mom panted and wheezed the whole way, even with the aid of additional oxygen. Sarah ran ahead to pull up the car, and we eased Mom into the front seat with her oversized purse and portable oxygen tank.

I opened the back door and leaned in to set the container of leftovers on the seat next to me. My rear end barely touched the leather when Sarah, all too aware of the time, threw the sedan in reverse and gunned the engine. The car lurched backward before I had even closed the passenger door. I was thrust headlong into the back seat. A blip of complete silence filled the air. Mom sat in a mild state of shock, and I was laughing so hard that no sound came out of my mouth. Within seconds, hysterical laughter erupted.

That birthday ended up being my mom's last one here on earth. Though she didn't get to celebrate Dineo's first birthday with us in person, I got to be with Mom for her last.

And it was grace.

CHAPTER 21

GRIEF

"By day the LORD directs his love, at night his song is with me—a prayer to the God of my life."

—Psalm 42:8

In early 2011, four years after Mom's re-diagnosis and less than six months after my visit to Michigan for her fifty-ninth birthday, Mom's health nose-dived. I lost count of how many times she changed chemotherapy drugs over those forty-eight months. One strain seemed to work for a bit, until the cancer cells figured it out, and prevailed. Another option, and again, tests looked encouraging. For a while. Then the tumor marker count increased, and she'd switch to different treatment. Eventually the day arrived that we all knew was coming. She ran out of chemotherapy drugs to try.

The ink is faded in that chapter of my life, the one I've tried so vigorously to erase from the pages of my memory, to no avail. It's the chapter when I traveled from Africa with my mom's three precious grandchildren, and she exhaled.

Mom's friends later told me she was waiting for me. She held on until we arrived, then just couldn't hold on any longer. What a strange feeling, to be waited for. To think that a dying person could muster up enough self-will to persevere, if a goal were in sight. She wanted me there. She wanted both of her girls. She wanted her grandkids.

I started a blog when Mom's health began to severely decline, in hopes that writing would be an outlet for me to decompress the stress. After my arrival that day in June 2011, I wrote a post entitled, "Nothing." It was three lines long:

I thought that this blog might be able to help me process this journey.

I was wrong.

Nothing could help me to process this.

Back in Cape Town after six weeks in Michigan helping Mom settle into the Hospice House, I grieved new losses every day. One of the most profound was realizing Mom would never call me on the phone again. As the cancer took over her body, her hands and mind grew too shaky to dial the phone. I'd grown so accustomed to expecting her phone calls in my eight years living abroad. I felt cut off from her, even though she was still alive. Death came as an erosion, like the sand dunes that cascade down toward Lake Michigan. I stood on the bank and watched while the gulf between my mom and me grew wider as she drifted away, silent on the waves.

The phone calls and emails that did come from Sarah each day only held more bad news. More side effects. More complications. Spreading numbness and tingling in Mom's hands and feet. Blurred vision. Slurred speech. Bed sores. Infections.

When the calendar flipped to September, three weeks after returning to Cape Town, I knew we were on the last lap. Like any long-distance race, the end was the most tiring part. I could hardly feel my legs, I was so tired of running this dreadful marathon. Temptation tapped me on the shoulder: "Just give up. Just collapse onto the curb and forfeit your medal. You don't deserve to finish well." The burning in my thighs and the ache in my chest told me to bow out of the competition against both cancer and unbelief—but something greater spurred me on. The voice of Hebrews 12 spoke louder than the whispers: "Let us run with perseverance the race marked out for us. Let us fix our eyes on Jesus, the author and perfecter of our faith" (12:1-2). Locking eyes on the One who endured the cross, I bent down and double-tied my shoes so I wouldn't trip over my own laces in the final stretch.

By September 4, I had packed my suitcase to fly home for the imminent funeral. The last time I had packed a bag ahead of time was six years earlier, when I expected my first child to be born any day. On that occasion, I packed in anticipation of giving birth to my daughter and witnessing her first breath into mortality. This time, I packed in anticipation of the one who gave birth to me taking her first breath into immortality. The indeterminate timing was enough to make me lose my mind.

Then I thought of another who waits for a day He doesn't know. The Bible says that not even Jesus knows the day on which He will return—only the Father knows (Matt. 24:36; Mark 13:32). The promise is there—He *will* come, He *is* coming, He just doesn't know when. I felt a strange camaraderie in my own waiting. Jesus's bags may be packed like mine. As I sat waiting with Him, I could only pray, "Come, Lord Jesus. Come."

One Saturday in mid-September, Sarah took her computer to Mom's Hospice room so we could Skype. When the camera focused in on Mom's face, I couldn't believe how much her appearance had changed in just a few short weeks. The cancerous fluid continued to increase, causing Mom's entire body to swell, including her face. She lay stiff and propped up in her bed, still wearing her robe—unusual for one who insisted on getting dressed every day. She looked so uncomfortable. The conversation didn't last long. Her speech slurred, and the kids noticed. They looked at me with furrowed brows, wondering what happened to the grandma they knew and loved. I couldn't bear it. When we ended the call, I couldn't erase the image of Mom's puffed up face from my mind. It hurt more than words could describe to see her suffering like that—and yet I knew it would hurt even more when I couldn't see her on the webcam ever again. Still, it didn't seem fair to make her pain linger for mine to be tempered.

I told the kids to go play outside. When they disappeared out of sight, I crumpled to the floor and pleaded, "God, just take her. Take her now. I can't stand it any longer. Please just take her now." I cried until the tears ran dry.

The rest of the week, my nerves were just about shot. I gasped every time the phone rang, my pulse pounding in my throat. I thought I was going to have a heart attack, I was so stressed waiting for "the call."

My poor husband never knew what he'd find when he came home from work. Some nights I wanted to curl up in bed and drown myself in a tub of ice cream. Most days I was ready to hire a nanny and hibernate until the whole nightmare was over. But every once in a while, I steeled myself enough to push through the pain. In those moments, any hint of sympathy grated on me. The more people who fussed over me and told me how miserable I must feel, the more miserable I actually felt.

On one such afternoon when Kagiso got home, he could see that I was struggling. Without telling me, he kindly canceled his evening appointments to be with me. Instead of being grateful, I was irked. I didn't want to be coddled. I didn't want to be treated like I was about to break. It was too late for that. I just needed him to bend down and retie my shoelaces so I could get on with it. Grief and self-defense were such temperamental siblings—best friends one minute, sworn enemies the next.

To remain sane, I started going to the gym more frequently. I climbed onto a treadmill and just ran. And I am *not* a runner. But I ran anyway, because it felt right to run and run and try to escape from it all. The tread-mills at our gym faced windows that opened into a court-yard surrounded by tall apartment buildings on three sides. I looked up at the apartments as I jogged, pretend-ing I could run right into the lives of the people who lived there. Maybe I could hang their laundry on the balconies instead of my own.

But I couldn't escape. As much as I wanted to, I couldn't turn back, couldn't slip into someone else's life for a while. Instead I wiped the sweat from my forehead and accepted the truth that God had assigned me my portion and my cup; He had made my lot secure (Ps. 16:5). Deep down, even though it chafed against my fickle emotions, I knew I had to trust and believe that "whatever my lot, Thou hast taught me to say, 'It is well, it is well with my soul.'"[1]

My kids struggled being back in Cape Town too. They missed Grandma. They didn't understand why they couldn't talk to her on the phone anymore. They missed the luxuries of America. I saw my own homesickness in them. So we talked about the aches, and we talked about the homesickness. And we remembered that we're supposed to be homesick no matter where we live, because we're not home yet.

CHAPTER 22

GONE

*"For this God is our God for ever and ever;
he will be our guide even to the end."*

—Psalm 48:14

I hadn't been sleeping much at all, but on the night of September 22, sleep was completely elusive. It was as if the tight coils in my shoulders knew it was going to happen, even though I'd been expecting it for weeks. A couple of days earlier, Mom had slipped into a semiconscious state. The nurses didn't call it a coma, but she was sleeping all the time. Not eating. Not talking.

The end was near.

I sat up late into the night, putzing around on my computer, desperately seeking distraction. Finally, around two o'clock in the morning, my eyes glazed over and the lines on my computer screen blurred together. Sleep was within reach. I shuffled from the kitchen down the long, silent hallway to the master bedroom. My head hit the pillow for just over three hours until the high-pitched ring of the cordless landline phone bolted me awake.

"Get the phone."

The words shot out of my mouth as quickly as my head shot off the pillow. There was no "Will you please?" Just a command. I knew why it was ringing, and I couldn't do it. I couldn't bring myself to answer and hear the words "Mom is dead."

Kagiso fumbled for the phone as my own hand instinctively reached for the wall, as if its stability would settle my pounding pulse. I needed to be grounded. I needed something to steady myself, even though I was still in bed.

The digital clock read five-something in the morning. Years of mentally calculating the different time zones told me it was 11-something at night in Michigan. I could hear my sister's voice through the phone as Kagiso held it to his ear in the dark. She wasn't crying.

The words I could make out were not enough to confirm my fears, but only to raise more questions. Eventually Kagiso handed me the phone.

"Hey." My heart beat loud into the receiver while Sarah feigned an upbeat tone, calm and collected. "The Hospice nurse called. She says Mom is close to the end. Apparently there are certain signs the nurses know to watch for, and Mom is demonstrating several of them. She's restless and her breathing has changed. They called and said I should come. Kent and I are on our way there now. I was wondering if you'd like me to call you back when we get there and hold the phone to her ear so you can say good-bye."

I had no idea what I would say or even if Mom would be able to hear me, but I nodded okay through welled up tears. Kagiso took the phone to convey the message.

I leaned against the wall in bed as the minutes ticked by in the darkness of that September morning. Six weeks had passed since we landed back in Cape Town. Six weeks of wondering whether today would be the day. The phone rang again. I answered it myself, expecting Sarah to tell me she was holding the phone to Mom's ear.

"She's gone. We were too late."

If I hadn't been sitting down, I think I would've fallen over. Even though I knew it was coming, the shock stabbed me. She was supposed to be alive so I could say something. But she was gone.

It was over.

I tried to swallow my shock, but it escaped in a half gasp, half sob. Moments passed as Sarah and I let the first tears find their way down our cheeks in silence.

"Okay," I whispered. "I'll get on the first flight I can find. I'll be there as soon as I can. Get some sleep, you must be exhausted."

"I'm okay," Sarah assured me, blowing her nose.

We exchanged a few more words, the transatlantic phone cables binding our broken hearts together. After hanging up the phone, I curled into a fetal position on the carpeted floor and rocked back and forth until the anguish ran dry. Kagiso knew me well enough to leave me alone. Instead he dialed the phone to call his own mom with the heavy news.

For so many months leading up to that moment, I spent my days and nights nestled in the clutches of fear. Terrified that today would be the day. Then early that Friday morning I woke up, and it was gone. And I just sat there, rocking like a toddler on the cold floor. Abandoned by the fear that held me close for so long.

Then—unexpectedly—a blanket of relief. Not relief that Mom was gone. Relief at the awareness that *nothing more could happen to her.* Nothing more could go wrong.

I swiped my hand across my wet cheeks and blew my nose in a tissue, attempting to pull myself together. My mind fogged as I tried to process reality. The kids were still asleep. I got up from the carpet, opened the bedroom door, and tiptoed down the hallway. As soon as I stepped into the kitchen, a shrill beeping sounded. In my frazzled state, I completely forgot to deactivate the house alarm. We set it every night before bed to detect movement in any part of the house beyond the bedrooms.

So much for waiting to tell the kids. They emerged, groggy-eyed and confused, from their bedrooms. Seeing my red, swollen face, they asked, "What's wrong?" We corralled them to our bed while I tried to heave the lump of dread out of the pit of my stomach. The thought of breaking their hearts with the news crushed me.

Tears flowed into a shared ocean of sorrow. The lone tissue box made the rounds from one snotty nose to the next as we sniffled and sobbed out the ripples of immense loss. "She was like the best person in our family!" Dineo wailed. And she couldn't have been more right.

"Guys, I'm going to have to fly to Michigan by myself for the funeral, okay?" I explained. "Dad will take you to Ouma's house. She'll look after you while I'm gone." They nodded, watching me with hollow eyes. I hated leaving them in such a tender state, but there was no other way. Kagiso helped them pack their things while I got myself as ready as possible. I stood in a hot shower and let the grief cascade down my shoulders. I watched it pool at my feet. If only it would disappear down the drain. If only it would make me feel clean.

The next hours blurred into phone calls, packing, and friends breezing through with arms full of sympathy and food. By late afternoon I was making my way through airport security.

Ever since my parents divorced when I was seven years old, my mom was the cement that held up our home. She became the foundation of the family, raising Sarah and me as a single parent. Anyone who knew her would say that we were her everything. She talked about us everywhere she went—the bank, the post office, the grocery store. She poured her life into her daughters, instilling quiet Christian values and not-so-quiet traditions into the fiber of our beings.

Mom was the bond that held our home together. And now she was gone.

Seven years before I sat on the plane that fateful day, I spoke marriage vows that forged a new home. Granted, it was in a foreign land where even simple acts proved to be a burden. My accent betrayed me with every word, revealing that I was out of place. As much as I tried to stretch out the fabric of Cape Town, it always felt a bit tight, like jeans that just came out of the tumble dryer. But with my vows, I bid America farewell and committed to South Africa and her people. Despite our differences, I determined to make her my home.

Just as my feet started to feel anchored to South Africa as my adopted home turf, half a world away, it was as if the tectonic plates of the earth shifted—and I felt it in my core. The foundation no longer felt firm. I was standing on unstable ground. The most faithful woman I knew would no longer welcome me home.

So was I heading home? Or not? The conflicting voices in my head kickstarted a long-lasting soul search: *Where was my home now?*

CHAPTER 23

GOOD-BYE

"Give ear, O LORD, to my prayer;
listen to my plea for grace. In the day of my trouble
I call upon you, for you answer me."

—Psalm 86:6–7 ESV

It was the day I had dreaded more than any other. The day we buried my mom. Two days prior, Sarah and I endured four hours of visitation, during which Mom's friends and acquaintances came from near and far to give condolences. My dad was there with Angela. They stayed for the whole visitation period, all the way to the end, and the funeral service too. It was like a silent peace offering. A quiet apology, speaking volumes from a man of few words. And I felt the scab of an age-old wound start to fade.

The morning before the funeral, I sent a mass email to a number of friends:

Yesterday we had four hours of 'visitation,' during which people came to pay their respects. While it was emotionally draining, it was healing and therapeutic in many ways as well. I wish I could have recorded all the testimonies that were shared about Mom. We had considered having an open mic at the memorial service for people to talk about Mom, but our pastor said, "I might consider that for other funerals, but this was your mother. We would be here for days."

Even one of Mom's surgeons came to give his condolences. He said, "I hardly ever do this for my patients, but your mom was something else." And she really was. Others talked about how they would go to visit her, hoping to be an encouragement to her in her suffering, and instead they themselves would come out feeling uplifted by Mom. That's just who she was. Another commented, "You only had to meet her once to recognize just how special she was."

A longtime family friend said through tears, "I know your mom is a whole lot better now, but the rest of the world is a whole lot worse."

I can't tell you how many people said to me, "You had the BEST mom. You really did." And they weren't saying it in the cliché sense, but almost as if they were jealous that we had been so privileged. All I could do was nod; they didn't have to persuade me.

Mom was not afraid to die. She was eager to meet her Lord. But she was worried about leaving my sister and me behind. As I looked around the room yesterday, I realized just how tightly wrapped we are in an intricate cocoon of love and support. And that cocoon was spun by Mom, through her joyful labor of love and encouragement to so many over the years, out of service to her King.

It seemed fitting that the Lord took my mom during autumn. Laying on the beach in summer was her ultimate enjoyment, but she was also enamored with the changing leaves in the fall. In her lifetime, Mom captured countless displays with her camera—fiery reds, oranges, and yellows. Two years after she passed away, I found burgundy maple leaves pressed between the pages of her favorite cookbook. She loved the colors so much, she even sent dried leaves to me in Cape Town—more than once.

But it also seemed appropriate to bury her in late September because the grass wouldn't grow over her casket until after the snow melted. In my opinion, the grass should never grow back. The wet soil of the grave should never be covered. If it did, it would mean that life had moved on—and I didn't know how it could. How the rawness of the wound could ever scab over with a layer of new life.

Bitter wind bit at my legs that day. I shivered from the inside out and scolded myself for not buying a warmer outfit. My knee-length dress and black cardigan weren't enough to cover my emptiness. Even the trees shivered in shared sorrow, shedding crimson and gold tears that wafted through the frigid air. They landed, soundless, on the ground. Dust to dust. I looked up and saw the dwindling flame of bright leaves. Orange embers reminded me of Moses's awe when God appeared to him in a burning bush (Exod. 3). That same God, the one called "I AM," the one who is always present—He was present in the cemetery, too, for "precious in the sight of the LORD is the death of his saints" (Ps. 116:15 ESV).

The funeral home set up a white canopy over the grave site, with a row of three or four chairs underneath. My ninety-two-year-old grandma was there—a rare outing from the Alzheimer's unit in her assisted living facility. Grandma had good days and not-as-good days with her dementia and her ability to remember things and understand what was going on—but that day, she knew.

She knew exactly what was happening, and it wrecked her.

To watch a rectangular wooden casket get lowered into the ground and know that it contained the body of her firstborn, her eldest daughter—it was too much for her to bear. She tried desperately to hold in her sobs, but they escaped in broken, gurgling chokes. Someone draped a blanket around her shoulders while Sarah and I flanked her on both sides. I leaned in and rubbed her arm, offered sips of bottled water, and exchanged used tissues for clean ones. I was so preoccupied by my grandma's weeping that my own grief was momentarily laid aside.

In the moments I anticipated would be the hardest of my life, the Lord's grace showed up in the disguise of distraction. He made me so focused on consoling my grandma that I nearly forgot the nauseating throb of my own broken heart. His promise had held true. His grace was sufficient.

After the burial, we had some time before the funeral started, so we went back to Sarah's house. Relatives watched television and ate snacks, but I went upstairs to lie down. I tried to sleep, but I was too cold. I couldn't stop shivering, even under several blankets. Even my bones convulsed in silent sobs.

Somehow I managed to get dressed and to the church for the funeral, cushioned by my dearest relatives. The inner circle of immediate family congregated in a private gathering space, waiting for other attendees to find seats before we filed down the aisle to the front rows. As we waited, the somber conversation turned to one of the last times we had all gathered in the same church—for my wedding, seven years earlier.

My mom's brother, Tom, and brother-in-law, Ross, who positively crack me up every time we're together, started in on a story I'd never heard from that day. "Right after the ceremony, Tom and I were getting ready to drive you and Kagiso to the reception, and I spilled mustard on my tie!" Ross said. "I didn't have any way to clean it, so I used brake fluid to get the stain out!"

At the church. On my wedding day. I knew nothing of this, until that afternoon as we sat waiting for my mom's funeral to begin. Of course by that stage, we were all howling and kept laughing as my uncle concluded, "The stain came out . . . the only problem was the *smell*!" I looked around the room. It felt scandalous to wipe tears of *laughter* from the corner of my eyes, minutes before a funeral. *My mother's funeral.* Like the autumn leaves on that cloudy day, God gave a splash of color in the midst of the gray.

Moments later, our pastor corralled our thoughts toward the service and told us to line up near the back door. I suddenly felt so abruptly alone, without dad, mom, or husband near me. I gripped my uncle's elbow and pleaded, "Will you sit next to me?"

"Of course," he replied. I needed a sturdy pillar to lean on. As it turned out, we took turns holding each other up.

Just before we formed a procession to enter the sanctuary, our pastor announced, "Okay, here we go. And I want you to sing the songs with gusto! She would've wanted that!" It was true. My mom had a lot of time to think about her own funeral, and she'd insisted that there be lots of singing. Joyful singing. She knew exactly where she was going when she died—and to her, that was reason to rejoice.

It sounded like a good idea, but there was just one problem: in my past experiences at funerals, the lump in my throat had grown so large I couldn't even swallow, let alone get any sound to come out. How much more so during my own mother's funeral? But to my surprise, the Lord again gave grace. When the music started, I stood there in the front row, looked straight up at the huge wooden cross hanging in the front of our church, and I sang. I even smiled while I sang, because "soon and very soon, we are going to see the King."[1] It was a smile on a tear-stained face, but it was a genuine smile, as I pictured the infinite joy my mom was experiencing at that very moment, doing what she loved best for all eternity.

A few days after the funeral, Sarah and I needed to get away. Our emotional reserves were depleted. We had to find a place to refuel, so we packed the car and headed five hours north to Petoskey, Michigan, to stay with Kent's brother, Drew. We took the scenic route along the lakeshore, driving slow and stopping often, just because. I doubt my foot could've pressed any harder on the gas pedal, even if I'd tried. We passed farm stands on the side of the road and talked about apple picking and pumpkins and hot cider. Anything but Mom. And yet, I couldn't think about any of those things without her invading every memory.

Loss had a way of setting everything in slow motion. Time dawdled as Sarah and I strolled in and out of quaint shops, pausing in boutiques to try on dresses we couldn't afford, pretending we were whole. I snapped pictures of the changing autumn leaves that painted color into the edge of Lake Michigan and silently confessed I was just like my mom.

The new scenery felt like a fresh start. I watched leaves float to the ground and wished my anguish could fall with them. But the pain was still fresh and green and very much alive.

Drew welcomed us with gentle hugs and few words. He knew we were fragile, and treated us so. His house was a safe haven. Nobody had any expectations of me there. Sarah and I spent a couple nights on Drew's pull-out couch, watching baseball, eating pizza, and dancing to *Michael Jackson: The Experience* on the Nintendo Wii. Anything for distraction. We avoided talk about past or future. We just paused, trying to relearn how to breathe.

On Saturday morning, Sarah took a nap while I went for a walk. The sky was blue, the sun shining, the wind strong. I had to keep walking. If I stopped, the weight of reality pressed heavy against my chest. By moving, I stayed one step ahead of it, preoccupied by motion. I followed the road down to Lake Michigan and found myself on the Petoskey pier. I thought about reckless friends pier-jumping in high school and tried to forget why I was there, standing on a shoreline in North America while my husband and kids could smell Atlantic salt several time zones away. My hair whipped across my face. The wind was so powerful, I had to step with purpose to keep from losing my balance. To my left, the waves were choppy and volatile. Immediately to the right of the pier, the water's surface was strangely smooth and flat. No waves. No churning. Just calm.

The contrast made me think of my position in Christ. If I didn't have Him, I would've been on the left side of the pier, floundering in rough waters. Overcome. But because of Jesus, I was on the calm side, protected even in the strongest of winds. In the years that my mom suffered, I often felt as if the waves swelled out of control. But in hindsight, I saw how God's power extended even over wind and waves, cancer cells and chemotherapy. That blustery day on the Petoskey pier, God reminded me that He is my refuge. Because I'm hidden in the shadow of the Rock, I knew I was safe in Him, no matter what storm may come.

The next morning, I walked into a church I'd never been in before. I didn't know it, and it didn't know me. I found it surprisingly freeing to be anonymous, even if only for an hour. There was something about being able to worship unhindered, without a past or present identity. I didn't have to share my story. I wasn't labeled as The One Who Just Lost Her Mom. Nobody knew anything about my baggage. I could just be.

But it didn't last long. Sarah and I had to get back in the car to drive back to Holland. Back to real life. Leaving Petoskey was hard. I wanted to stay hidden, away from the pain. I wanted to remain unnoticed. Unknown. I could've slipped into that community without my history. I wanted to start a new story—but God had other plans. He didn't give me a new story to write, He gave me *this* one. "This is my story. This is my song." We sang the lyrics of "Blessed Assurance" at my mom's funeral. It was time to live them.

When Sarah and I got back from Petoskey, we were smacked in the face with a condo full of stuff to be emptied. Every time I opened the door to Mom's condo after she died, I wanted to throw up. More than once, when I was supposed to be sorting, tossing, and packing, I crumpled to the floor in tears. At one point, I lifted a purple

T-shirt Mom got at a Relay for Life event. Across the back, bold, white letters spelled out SURVIVOR. I wanted to burn that shirt because she wasn't. She hadn't.

Then I remembered the speech I had written for her funeral. Sarah read the speech aloud so eloquently and bravely on my behalf. In it I had written that contrary to popular opinion and all external appearances, Mom *had* won the fight. She had won because Jesus had won, and she was His.

She won—but my gosh, why did it have to hurt so badly?

The pain came something fierce when one of my mom's best friends showed up with a van full of white bags with the blue Hospice logo printed across each one. I had almost forgotten about everything left behind in Mom's room when she died. This angel of a friend went in afterward and packed up all of Mom's belongings, folding each item with great care. As she deposited the bags in Sarah's entryway, a fresh wave of sorrow swept over me. Mom's purple, velour zip-up jacket rested on top of one of the bags. The same jacket I helped Mom put on over her nightgown when she was too weak to let me change her clothes the day we waited for the paramedics to wheel her out of her condo for the last time. The same purple jacket that warmed me as I napped in her far-too-heavily-air-conditioned Hospice room after we moved her in. The jacket came back to us that day, the day her belongings no longer had an owner, the day her jacket was formless and empty, without a body to give it shape. I took the jacket upstairs, fell into a heap on the carpet, and cried myself to sleep.

The day dawned when Mom's condo had to be empty. We scheduled a local charity to come haul away everything that was left after I had filled a storage unit with items I wanted to keep for when Kagiso, the kids, and I moved to Michigan four months later. A considerable amount remained, including the blue leather couch, numerous boxes and Rubbermaid totes, lamps, and an artificial tree. Sarah and I surveyed the scene and realized it was a lot to manage on our own. We needed more manpower. Neither of our husbands were there, and none of the friends we called could help. We waited for the truck to arrive, presuming the drivers would carry the heaviest pieces of furniture down the flight of stairs.

A big white truck pulled up. Two thin, elderly men emerged from the front. My raised eyebrows met Sarah's: *Are you serious?* We pursed our lips to muffle the laughter. If not suppressed giggles, it would've been tears. There was no way that these sweet old men would be able to lug all the furniture, boxes, and garbage bags down a flight of stairs and onto the truck themselves. Sarah pulled out her cell phone and frantically tried to call in backup, but failed to round up any last-minute recruits. So we rolled up our sleeves, put on our brave faces, and got to work, huffing and puffing and cursing all earthly possessions.

We grunted the blue leather couch through the hallway, down the stairs, and out the door. We sweated up and down the staircase, heaving loads into the truck. When we finally finished, we thanked the gray-haired men for their labor. They closed up the back of the truck, climbed into the front seats, and drove away with a generation of memories and a chunk of my heart. I stood in the parking lot and blinked back tears—yet another unshed good-bye.

Like Mom's body, all that was left of the condo was a hollow shell. The shell remained, but the spirit was gone.

That moment haunted me for weeks afterward. Whenever I saw the back of that truck in my mind, my stomach churned a little. The lesson played on repeat: Hold material things loosely. Even if they're sentimental, they're temporary. When I die, I can't take anything with me.

And yet, I'll have everything I need.

After my mom died, I started thinking a lot more about heaven. On one particularly beautiful day, I caught myself thinking, "Oh, what a pity that Mom's missing such a glorious day. She would have loved this blue sky and sunshine." Then I realized my fallacy—Mom was in an infinitely better place. This life is but a shadow.

Again, I would drive past one of Mom's favorite restaurants and think, "How sad that she'll never be able to eat chicken pad thai from Thai Palace or Mongolian beef from Mr. You's Chinese take-out." Then God reminded me that even the best Chinese buffet on earth has nothing on heaven's buffet.

One afternoon, a disturbing question smacked me between the eyes: do I care more about being reunited with Mom in heaven than I care about being with God? My conscience accused me. More questions followed on the heels of the first: Why have I only *really* started taking an interest in heaven after knowing my mom was there? Why haven't I cared as much before? Why hadn't all those other deaths in years past—my best friend's mom in sixth grade, my neighbor in high school, and several others—prompted the same desire and longing in my heart? Even if nobody else were there, shouldn't my longing for heaven be for God alone, and nothing more?

I once saw the most remarkable video of an infant, just minutes after birth. She had been placed skin-to-skin on her mother's abdomen, shock of black hair still matted with remnants of amniotic fluid. With eyes clenched shut, the newborn managed to inch her way upward, squirming like a worm. Slowly, gradually, this baby squirmed and grunted along her mother's skin until she found the source of the milk—and she began to drink.

Deep down, in the hollows of our own hearts, we know there is milk to be found. We can smell it. We thirst for it. God has planted in us a homing device that causes us to squirm and grunt on our bellies in the darkness until we find the source of Living Water. Until we find the Light. Until we find Home.

Before leaving Michigan to go back to Cape Town, I went to say good-bye to my grandma at her nursing home. I found her in the dining room, finishing the last bites of her supper. Grandma's face lit up in recognition when she saw me. I couldn't help but have a flashback to the anguish she had endured days before. I looked at her with sympathy, ready to tread carefully with my words.

"Hi, Grandma!"

"Well, hi! It sure is good to see you! Maybe now they'll let me leave this table without finishing my applesauce. They always make it too tart."

I laughed. "Well, nobody can make applesauce as well as you do, Gram." She feigned humility, but the sparkle in her eyes betrayed her. I looked down at her hands resting on the table, and I saw Dineo's hands. And it struck me—we're all passing down, passing on, passing away. God gave the baton of faith to my grandma, who passed it down to my mom. She passed it on to me, and now it was my turn to pass that same gift of the gospel to the next generation.

After we chatted for a while, Grandma announced, "Your mom hasn't been here for a while."

My breath caught in my throat. *She didn't remember.*

I swallowed hard before admitting, "Yeah. I know."

I didn't have the heart to say anything more. Instead, I silently thanked God for letting her forget the nightmare. And I wished He would do the same for me.

Sixteen days after my mom died, I had to return to South Africa. On the day of my departure, I posted on my blog:

I leave today. And I really hate good-byes.

It used to be that Mom was always, always, always the one who drove us to the airport, without fail. Then one time she was too sick to take us, so we said good-bye to her at her house. With the next couple of trips, we got used to the idea, but the last time, we left her in her hospice room.

This time, the good-bye was entirely different. This time, I drove down the road, got out of my car, walked across some wet grass and said good-bye to a rectangle of fresh dirt.

The past five times I've had to say good-bye, I always wondered whether I would see her again. Now I have the answer.

And the answer is yes.

Yes, I will see her again.

When I knelt on the cold, hard earth that October morning, I knew my mom wasn't there. I knew I couldn't say good-bye to her anymore. Before I left, I walked slowly up and down the rows of headstones, reading about those who had gone before. My heart snapped into fresh pieces. Among the saddest were the four-year-old girl, the forty-year-old mother who left behind a husband and four children, and the two sisters, ages twenty and twenty-one, who had died on the same day. I couldn't imagine the depth of those losses.

Walking through a cemetery does one thing for me, without fail: it reminds me, with stark tangibility, that this is not our home. This life is not forever. We're only passing through.

Maybe instead of saying good-bye, I should've said, "See you when I get home."

CHAPTER 24

HOME

*"Teach me your way, O LORD, that I may walk in
your truth; unite my heart to fear your name.
I give thanks to you, O Lord my God, with my whole
heart, and I will glorify your name forever."*

—Psalm 86:11–12 ESV

The day I left Sarah behind seared me. I didn't want to go, but Kagiso and the kids needed me. That familiar torn feeling was the story of my life. I'd lived the better part of a decade in a state of taut-rope tension, since Mom first became ill. A vicious tug-of-war, with two sides of the Atlantic pulling with all their might, neither side willing to let go. My only consolation in leaving Sarah behind was the promise that we'd be moving to Michigan in a few short months.

I landed in Cape Town unprepared for the new normal. I had focused so much on the actual phone call and funeral that I hadn't steeled myself for the hardest

part of all—learning to function in this unknown territory. A reality where people didn't quite know what to
say, especially since they'd been repeating the same line,
"How's your mom?" for the past nine years. A reality where
the kids might accidentally forget that Grandma wasn't
there anymore and ask if they could Skype her. A reality
where Christmas presents didn't come in the mail any
longer. A new normal where the world kept turning, but
the axis had shifted and everything spun off-kilter.

Even the passage of time felt different. One span of
three weeks seemed like three months, while another felt
like yesterday. Sometimes I even forgot Mom was gone.
Weeks after she died, I turned to pick up the phone to tell
her about something cute Caleb had just done, before
realizing that I couldn't. Then I felt ridiculous, because
how could I possibly forget? After the trauma of the
decline and then her death and funeral, how could I not
remember? Apparently thirty-year-old habits die hard.

But how could I complain about her absence, when
I'd asked for it? Prayed for it, even? For the longest
time, I couldn't bear to ask God to take her home. I
regretted that prayer, later. I wanted her back. But the
Lord reminded me of the book *Stepping Heavenward*
by Elizabeth Prentiss, and the part where Elizabeth
temporarily wishes that her godly mother hadn't died.
Then she realizes how selfish it would be to desire her
mother's return to a world of pain and suffering, when
she was now enjoying paradise with God forever. The
thought softened the blow. A little.

Granted, in the days and weeks that immediately followed, the generic consolation, "At least you know she's

in a better place" did little to soothe the raw and gaping wound that bled from my soul. I knew she was with her Lord in glory. But still—she was gone. The hole in my heart remained empty. Kagiso bore with me patiently, giving me space when the tears fell.

The sting was bittersweet. I read somewhere that bittersweet is defined as "an outcome for something that was wished for but with unforeseen consequences." One of those unforeseen consequences of my mom's death was the lingering lull afterward. I didn't fully realize just how much anxiety and stress I had absorbed from the circumstances, nor how much it consumed me. When Mom died and all the prolonged stress was suddenly gone, there was an emptiness, a gap. An eerie quiet. No more email updates about her health. No more doctor's reports. No more pending test results. No more cheerful phone calls.

I knew the hollow feeling wouldn't last forever, but even that thought was disconcerting—as if she could be replaced. As if the void could be filled. Yet I knew deep down that the sun would shine again. She would want it to. Some describe bittersweet as "sweet with a bitter aftertaste." For me, it was "bitter with a sweet aftertaste." Bitter then, bitter now, but promised sweetness yet to come.

Getting myself to church became an act of willpower. Desire disappeared. I cried at every Sunday service, somewhere between the welcome and benediction. I felt the eyes staring at me. Burning a tattoo of embarrassment into my skin.

It took a long time to climb out of the wreckage of grief and shock. Over and over just as I was about to glimpse light, I slipped and fell back into the rubble. Death is a destructive force. It wreaks havoc in its wake.

Over the next several weeks, I thought back to a Ladies' Coffee Morning at my church that took place four months before my mom died. I had served as the MC, and had asked a college-aged friend of mine to share her story. She stood up to the podium, microphone amplifying her voice throughout the church hall. She told us how her mom had died recently. Suddenly. Unexpectedly. And how, when she had heard the news, she didn't know what she was going to do. How she was going to cope. How she would ever make it through the deep, dark valley. But she stood in front of that room full of women, captivated eyes fixed on her small frame, and she explained it simply: "It was grace. It was all grace. That's what got me through. I never thought it was possible, but He did it. It's still hard, and it probably always will be, but His grace is how I can face each day."

That's when the tears began. I couldn't contain them. They hovered on the brink of my eyelids and I tried not to blink, but they spilled over anyway. At the time, I was on the other side of her story, clinging with exhausted fingertips to my mom's life. This story of hers would soon become my own. But even as she spoke, I didn't believe it would be true for me. I knew the Bible said His grace was sufficient, but I had deemed myself an exception to the rule. I doubted the grace of God.

Four months later, my mom died. And what I never expected, happened. God carried me. He caused me to keep my composure as I traveled alone to the funeral. He gave me the strength to make it through the visitation and the memorial service. He helped me to console my grandma at the grave site as we watched the casket lower into the ground. He gave me a clear mind to make decisions that had to be made, like which belongings we would keep, and which verse should be inscribed on the gravestone.

It was awful and it was grace, all at the same time. And it's still grace, with every day that stabs and stings and sleeps and wakes. I doubted, and God proved me wrong. I was faithless, and God was faithful (2 Tim. 2:13). And now, I can stand with my friend, my fellow motherless daughter, and testify myself that His grace *is* sufficient. His power *is* made perfect in weakness (2 Cor. 12:9). To God be the glory.

Less than a month after she died would have been my mom's sixtieth birthday. Between the heavy fog of grief and the tears that flooded my eyes, I couldn't see a thing. I cried over every incident that day, great or small—over the people who remembered, and those who forgot.

Our beloved pastor in Cape Town sent me an email that evening:

Dear Kate, I know today must have had its sadness. There is one overwhelming thought which comes to mind: Your mom is 60 today, and more alive than she has ever been! She may not be present to celebrate it with you all, but she is in the Lord's presence, and when she has cele-brated her 10 millionth birthday would have only begun to fathom the depths of joy and delight, richest, deepest fellowship, beauty, grace, and wisdom of what it means to dwell as a daughter of our Lord in His presence with His people forevermore, eternally. I suppose as I've watched my dad's weakness and frailty these last few weeks, I'm more aware and grateful than ever before that heaven is the home of God's people and that whatever sadness and pain there might be here cannot begin to compare with the joy of being at home with the Lord. Your mom now knows that—thank the Lord Jesus! Please pray that my dad will soon know that too.

In the Lord's mercy, our pastor's prayer request was granted less than a year after this was written. His dad now indeed knows the richness and wonder of heaven as his eternal home. Even when the sun slips below the horizon, we know it's still there. And because God is faithful, we know we'll see it again, shining in all its radiant glory, in the new tomorrow. Our earthly nature whispers lies that this is our only home. That death is the end. It's only the beginning. Only then will the wanderings of painful toil, heartaches, and heartbreaks be over, and believers in Christ will finally be home.

In November 2011, two months after my mom died and two months before the Johnsons were due to return to their home in Cape Town, we hit another road block in our attempts to move to America. Some of the South African paperwork required for Kabelo to apply for a U.S. green card would take a full year to obtain. My heart sank: *Now what will we do?* We had already given away all our furniture, fully expecting to make the seamless transition from the Johnsons' furnished home to a new landing place in the States. With no other choice, we began to pack up our belongings, not knowing where we would unzip our suitcases after the Johnsons returned in a handful of weeks.

I called Sarah to break the news. After the persistent setbacks, she and I both wondered if we would ever live in the same country again. The storage unit full of Mom's stuff would sit untouched, sucking our money every month for much longer than I had anticipated when I slammed the garage door shut after Mom's funeral. After months of preparation, the kids had to make major mental shifts. "What? We're not leaving anymore? Why not? Where are we going to live?" Only the Lord knew.

After a few weeks of uncertainty, the Lord provided another rental down the street. Various friends and acquaintances pooled resources to furnish our new abode. A mattress here, a fridge there. A dining room table and mismatched chairs. A makeshift couch and a scratched coffee table. Piece by piece, God pulled it together. One dear friend even spoiled us with brand new duvet covers for the kids' beds—a complete surprise that made them exclaim with joy.

The year was not wasted. We found dear friends in our new neighbors, friends with whom we could laugh and cry. We hosted another year of weekly Bible studies in our small living room, eager brothers and sisters huddled around tea, biscuits, and a shared love for the Word of God. As we continued to jump through the many hoops required for Kagiso and Kabelo's green card applications, we quietly wondered if we were making the right decision. Should we really leave?

Yes, it was time—but only for a little while. Lord willing, we would spend a few years in the States—just long enough for the kids to forge lasting, in-person relationships with my side of the family and get a feel for American culture—and then we would return to South Africa to minister long-term and fulfill Kagiso's lifelong dreams.

After piles of paperwork, money, and patience, we got the green light. It was time to move. My swirling emotions surprised me. As excited as I was to move to the States with Kagiso and the kids, I couldn't imagine living there without my mom. Right next to the excitement and apprehension sat a deep sense of loss over the family, friends, and culture we would leave behind.

On January 25, 2013, we hauled ten bulging suitcases through airport security and squeezed Kagiso's mom and a horde of trailing friends good-bye. The tears flowed freely from both sides. Until the moment I turned my back on her, I hadn't realized just how much Cape Town had become part of my identity. She was so much more than a place to land—she was a part of me.

Ten years prior, when I stepped onto that plane for my first ever flight to Cape Town, little did I know just how much life would change.

I was a few weeks shy of twenty-one, and my plan was to stay for five months. But just as my childhood stay in the renovated pump house stretched into a decade, what I thought would be a few months overseas morphed into ten and a half years. God's plan kept me there and stained my heart with Rooibos tea and red African soil.

Over ten years, I moved ten times, bookended by my initial move to South Africa, and then back again to West Michigan. Time and time again with each new rental apartment, each borrowed house, I desperately tried to convince myself that I was content. But the truth was, when I was here, I wanted to be there, and when I was there, I wanted to be here.

At first, all I wanted was to hang pictures on the walls without fear of our landlord inspecting the drywall at the end of our lease. To pound a nail into fresh paint and transform a bland house into my signature flavor. But after a chain of rented apartments and long-term house-sitting stints, I lost interest in making any effort. Knowing we'd be moving again soon stifled my desire to settle. Sometimes I didn't even bother to unwrap the scented candles from their swaths of newspaper. In the last few rentals, I even left the framed family photos tucked away in their Bubble Wrap, knowing that I would just have to rewrap them soon anyway. As we packed suitcases and boxes for the umpteenth time, I felt the burden of exile. The weight of my wandering.

Then finally, I understood. This whole life is a rental. This whole body of mine is a borrowed house. And sometimes it's a good thing to be discontent with where we are, because *this is not it*. It's a good thing to feel like we're not at home and to long for another, for permanence, for stability, because *we're not home yet*. Having been washed by the astounding grace of the cross, praise God, my citizenship is in heaven (Phil. 3:20).

My life sprawled out between the parentheses of two continents. This is living in the "in between"—between the fall and redemption, the already and the not yet, between hope's longing and fulfilment. Where time passes with the click of a mouse and drags like a whiny toddler down a grocery store aisle. Where graves are dug and happiness buried. Where bees and words sting, and hopes are ripped off like stubborn bandages. Where victory has been accomplished, but Christ has not yet returned.

God took my definition of home, tore it up, and tossed it out the passenger seat window, where it caught the southeaster, never to be seen again. He opened to that chapter of my soul where the ink is faded, the yellowed pages transparent from vigorous scribbles and constant erasing. For years, I obsessed over the pursuit of home. It always felt just out of reach. Visible, but unattainable. Now I see I had it all wrong. Home in its truest sense—my eternal home—is exactly the opposite. It's attainable but not visible. Attainable only because of Christ's work on the cross and His gift of faith to me. Invisible for a little while longer, "for what is seen is temporary, but what is unseen is eternal" (2 Cor. 4:18). It took me decades to figure out that home is partly about where

I'm from, yes—but home is far more about where I'm heading.[1]

Home is more than just a place—it's a promise.

Though my vision was clouded and confused for most of my childhood and young adult years, the Lord eventually etched a new prescription into my lenses. Over time, He took my nearsightedness and caused me to see far into the distance—all the way to the finish line. For a long time I floundered around, stooping to search for the scraps of that shredded definition of home that had been tossed to the wind. But all along, it was right there. The map was written on my heart, for upon it, He has set eternity (Eccles. 3:11).

After a full decade of seemingly continuous moves, I finally felt as though my hesitant and lax attitude toward "settling" gradually improved. Regardless of how long or short my stay might be in any particular abode, I've come to accept that each new place I land is one of the legs of my journey that the Lord has planned for me. He determined before time the exact periods and places I would live (Acts 17:26). Even if there may be several stops and a vast array of camping sites while I remain in my earthly tent, where I camp now is one more step allotted for me in the steady trip toward *home*. Every day, I'm one step closer to eternity.

I spent my life stretched and displaced, my love spread thin over multiple houses and vast lands. For decades, I lived with a divided heart. Mom's house versus Dad's house. Sports friends versus church friends. Faith versus doubt. Anger versus forgiveness. Godliness versus sin. Michigan versus Cape Town. Despair versus hope.

Then I came across a prayer in the Psalms, and wondered what it meant: "Teach me your way, LORD, that I may rely on your faithfulness; *give me an undivided heart*, that I may fear your name" (Ps. 86:11, NIV 2011, emphasis mine). *An undivided heart.* Was that possible? The fact that my affections sprawled so far and wide made me wonder: *Am I doing something wrong?* I felt I should be "all in" *somewhere*. But I cared about too many things, too many people, too many places. Surely an undivided heart meant a heart wholly devoted to God. Did loving God the way I was supposed to mean I shouldn't care so much about the pleasures in this world? Should I hurt less over all that is broken?

Or maybe it's all related. Perhaps having an undivided heart doesn't mean loving God *only*, at the expense of everything else. Maybe loving God's people, His places, His things, is just an extension of my love for Him. They're not mutually exclusive. Maybe if I acknowledge that He is over all and in all and through all, the scattered pieces of my heart become connected, and through Him, I am made whole.

God took the tug-of-war that waged in my soul, the thick rope that spanned across the ocean, and yanked from both sides. He cut it clean through the middle, somewhere over the depths of the Atlantic. And He made me look up. To see that the greatest and strongest pull is neither east nor west, neither here nor there. It's the heavenward pull.

It's the pull toward *home*.

I now know how to respond the next time someone asks me the simple question, "Are you heading home?"

Regardless of my earthly destination, and purely because of God's grace and Christ's sacrifice, I'll be able to answer with confidence, "Yes. Yes, I am."

Be still, my soul; the Lord is on thy side;
Bear patiently the cross of grief or pain;
Leave to thy God to order and provide;
In every change He faithful will remain.
Be still, my soul; thy best, thy heavenly, Friend
Through thorny ways leads to a joyful end.

—Catharina von Schlegel, "Be Still, My Soul"

NOTES

Chapter 7

1. Acts 17:24, Ephesians 3:12, Revelation 5:9, Philippians 4:19, Hebrews 11:16, Romans 14:11.

Chapter 8

1. The term "colored" in South Africa refers to certain people of mixed race and is not considered a derogatory term.

Chapter 21

1. Horatio G. Spafford, "It Is Well with My Soul," https://www.hymnal.net/en /hymn/h/341.

Chapter 23

1. Andraé Crouch, "Soon and Very Soon," http://hymnary.org/tune /soon_and_very_soon_crouch#Composer.

Chapter 24

1. This thought was inspired by Christie Purifoy's *Roots & Sky: A Journey Home in Four Seasons* (Grand Rapids: Revell, 2016).

ACKNOWLEDGMENTS

First and foremost to God, my Lord, Savior, Creator, Redeemer, and so much more. Without you I am nothing. Without you I have nothing. Through your grace and forgiveness you have given me the best and safest place to land—in you.

To acquisitions editor Andy Rogers, for answering the knock and letting this story in. Thank you for guarding it and escorting it until it found its place.

To executive editor Miranda Gardner, for your patience, discernment, guidance, and dedication. This book would not be what it is without your support and expertise.

To editor Joel Armstrong, for asking the hard questions and pushing me to dig deeper.

To editor Natalie Hanneman, for your wisdom, enthusiasm, superb work, careful attention to detail, and for nurturing both me and this story and carrying us both across the finish line.

To the entire team at Discovery House, for standing behind this book and its message, for your shared passion to make the gospel known, and for making the publication process such a delight.

To Ann Byle and Tim Beals at Credo Communications, for your guidance and support.

To my mom's friends, for the overwhelming kindness and care you poured out for years on end. You are a gift from above.

To those who gave sacrificially to cover airfare so my family and I could fly back and forth across the ocean:

You gave so much more than money. You etched stories and gratitude into this book and into my soul.

To the pastors who have shepherded me over the years: Thank you for faithfully showing me the beauty of Christ, holding out the Word of Life, and spurring me on in the race. Week after week you've stirred my anticipation for eternity, and for that I'm ever grateful.

To Jodi, for caring for my mom so well, and for the many hours you occupied my kids so I could attend writing conferences and make progress on this manuscript.

To Lynn Austin, first for over a decade of inspiration from your own writing, and more recently for the gracious encouragement in person. You are a blessing.

To Lisa-Jo Baker, baie baie dankie. Your writing, example, and ongoing enthusiasm have influenced me and this book more than I could express even over a whole afternoon dunking Ouma rusks into Five Roses tea.

To Asheritah, Katie, Patrice, Lisa, and so many other dear friends who have held me up in this journey—you always seemed to know exactly what I needed to hear at exactly the right time. Thank you for being sensitive to the Spirit and for being such a strong and faithful support system.

To the Five Minute Friday community, for spurring me on, holding me accountable, and for giving me a reason to write.

To my mom-in-law and to Kagiso's entire family, for welcoming me into your fold without hesitation, for loving me without reservation, and for allowing me to make your home my own. I thank God for you.

To my dad and Angela, for loving me in spite of myself.

To Kent and Sarah, for your faithful service both to Mom and the rest of us, for catching our tears, for making us laugh, for holding us up. We love you.

To Kabelo, Dineo, and Caleb, for your incredible patience and enthusiastic support. You're my biggest cheerleaders, and I love you more than you'll ever know. You've been split across cultures and continents, but my greatest prayer is that each of you would also find your home in Christ alone.

To Kagiso: You sacrificed more than anyone else in order for this book to see completion. Both my life and this story would be dismal without you. Thank you for your biblical leadership over our family, for bearing with me and all of my faults, for faithfully pointing me to Jesus, and for daily striving to love me as Christ loves the Church. Ke a go rata.

Enjoy this book? Help us get the word out!

Share a link to the book or
mention it on social media

Write a review on your blog, on a retailer site,
or on our website (dhp.org)

Pick up another copy to share with someone

Recommend this book for your
church, book club, or small group

Follow Discovery House on
social media and join the discussion

Contact us to share your thoughts:

 @discoveryhouse    @DiscoveryHouse

Discovery House
P.O. Box 3566
Grand Rapids, MI 49501 USA

Phone: 1-800-653-8333
Email: books@dhp.org
Web: dhp.org